THE FINKEL FAMILY MEMOIRS

THE FINKEL FAMILY MEMOIRS

By Murray I. Finkel, A. Allan Finkel,
Dotty Finkel, and Esther Kasden

With edits by Erica, Benjamin, and Andy Finkel

iUniverse, Inc.
New York   Bloomington

The Finkel Family Memoirs

iUniverse books may be ordered through booksellers or by contacting:

iUniverse
1663 Liberty Drive
Bloomington, IN 47403
www.iuniverse.com
1-800-Authors (1-800-288-4677)

ISBN: 978-1-4502-1392-9 (sc)
ISBN: 978-1-4502-1393-6 (dj)
ISBN: 978-1-4502-1394-3 (ebk)

Printed in the United States of America

iUniverse rev. date: 04/01/2010

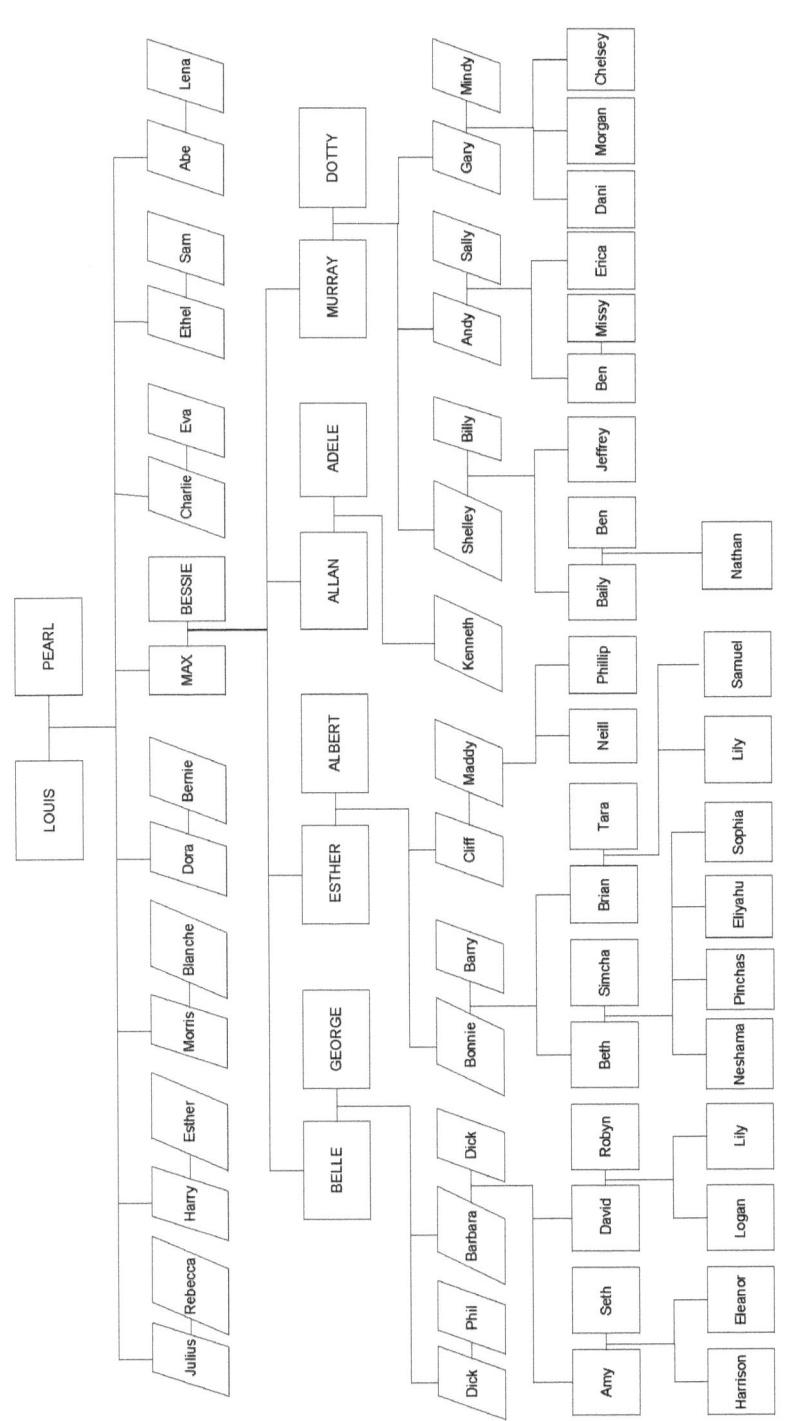

CONTENTS

Picture taken in Seltz, Russia 1907 - 1908

```
        MORRIS 14          HARRY 17          DORA 11
CHARLES 10   ABE 3   GRANDPA LOUIS 42   ETHEL 6   GRANDMA PEARL 49
     MAX and JULIUS were living in U.S
```

Finkel sisters and brothers in 1975
Taken at Bar Mitzvah of Martin Kobrin

```
  DORA          MORRIS  JULIUS   CHARLES   MAX   HARRY  ETHEL  ABE
```

Finkel family party (1950s)

IN THE BEGINNING

By Esther Kasden

M ax and Bessie Finkel were married on February 15, 1910. On February 16, Julius came from Europe and moved in with them. Then came Harry, followed by Morris and finally Dora. They all lived with Max and Bessie.

Dora and Bernie Davis had a large wedding in a catering hall on East Broadway in 1919. The couple then moved to an apartment in the Bronx at 868 Fox Street. The apartment was near an open-air movie theater, and we used to watch the movies from the fire escape. Harry and Esther were married in 1920 and moved to Rodney Street in the Williamsburg section of Brooklyn.

Our Grandma Pearl came to America with Charlie, Ethel, and Abie in 1921. Abie wore knickers at the time. Our Grandpa Louis was detained at the border in Hamburg for some reason. When he finally did come to America, he came first class.

We all went to meet him as he got off the ship. We had walked from our home on the East Side, because it was a religious holiday. We were lined up on both sides of the gateway. We saw a man with a beard carrying a straw suitcase with a teakettle and pots dangling from it. Bessie recognized him as Grandpa Louis from a photograph. She rushed over to him and called, "Shver, Shver," but he pushed her aside.

Our grandparents' first apartment was on Broome Street. When Max and Bessie moved to Brooklyn in August 1923, Grandma and Grandpa got them an apartment at 81 New Lots Avenue. When the upper apartment emptied at 330 New Lots Avenue, Louis, Pearl, Charlie, Ethel, and Abie moved in.

Charlie and Ethel were both married in 1925, and Sam Kobrin moved into the apartment with Abie, Louis, and Pearl.

MEMORIES

By Esther Kasden

285 Madison Street was a five-story walk-up tenement. There was a three-room, four-room, and five-room apartment on each floor. We lived in a four-room apartment on the fourth floor. The apartment entrance was also the kitchen. It contained a kitchen set and a "lunch" on which someone always slept. A "lunch" was like a sofa except it had only one arm and was probably made of leather. The kitchen led to the dining room, which had a dining room set and a folding double bed. There were also two bedrooms. When it was very hot, everyone slept on the roof.

Living in a tenement before and after World War I meant living in an apartment with a coal stove in the kitchen for heat. We were lucky. We had a bathroom in our apartment. Some buildings had a toilet in the hall of each floor. Others had outhouses in the backyards. When the four of us had to get dressed in the winter mornings, Mama would fill up the bathtub with hot water so we could get dressed in a nice, warm bathroom. Of course we all wore long johns.

One day Papa came home with a gadget to keep the bedroom warm. It fitted over the gas ceiling jet. It was shaped like a small Frisbee and had small holes in it like a burner on a stove for the flames to get out.

We all slept on perenes. They were comforters made of feathers, about a foot high, and very warm. Mama also improvised by putting pillows against the windows to keep out the cold and drafts.

I remember going into Mama's room after Allan was born. The window was completely frozen, but there were pillows against the windows. Belle and I were sent to the Tropp apartment on the fifth floor during the birth.

Aunt Dora, Abram, and Clara lived in our tenement at the same time. Our house was the gathering place for all their friends. Every Saturday night, Mama prepared herring and potatoes in jackets and baked cakes for everyone who gathered there. A great time was had by all. Papa was called Uncle Meyer or *Fetter* Meyer and Mama was called Tante Bessie or *Moome* Bessie. When we moved to New Lots Avenue, most of this group was married, but they always came to visit. They even came to visit years later in South Fallsburg. Mama and Papa, of course, were invited to all their weddings.

When we lived on the East Side, Belle went to a sleep-away camp for two weeks one summer. She went to the Edalia Home, which was run by the Educational Alliance. Most of the songs I learned as a child were songs that Belle sang when she came home. I also learned lots of songs when she went to Maxwell Training School for Teachers.

In 1918, after the United States had already entered the war, we all sang the following song:

HIP, HIP, the Kaiser's got the grippe,
WHY, WHY, because he's going to die,
WHERE, WHERE, under the chair,
WHEN, WHEN, at half past ten.

When Murray was about two- or three-years old, he would stand up on a table and sing "Found a Peanut".

Although Papa left for work very early, Mama was out of the house before 6 a.m. She would go to the bakery on Monroe Street to buy rolls for Papa's lunch.

Papa was a very conscientious worker. He worked until all hours. He worked all over the five boroughs, New Jersey, Sandy Hook, and wherever he could find a job.

We were one of the few families that had a telephone. One night, Papa was exceptionally late. In fact, it was close to midnight. We had no way of contacting anyone, because we never knew where he worked or whom he worked for. When he finally arrived home we chastised him for not calling us. His reply was, "I knew where I was."

It was my job to take Papa's saw to the sawman to get it sharpened. The sawman was always in a dreary room in the back of a house. It made no difference how far it was. Papa changed saw sharpeners frequently. I would get on my skates with the saw and seventy-five cents, and skate away.

Papa was very family-conscious. Since all his family was here, he was always sending money to my mother's family. Every time I skipped a grade, I was supposed to get five dollars. I skipped grade school five times, but I never saw the money. Each time the money was sent to my mother's relatives in Europe.

One day the telephone kept ringing in our house. All the *landsleit* were calling. They had seen an ad in the Jewish paper that Mama's nephew, who had moved to Israel, was looking for her. Contact was made, and Papa had a new place to send money. He sent money for a milking machine and a variety of other things the cousin needed. He also sent money and things needed by another cousin moving his family from Poland to Israel. Mama and Papa went to Israel for their fiftieth anniversary to meet these relatives.

I went to the library every Saturday morning. It was not enough for me, however, so Papa gave me money weekly to buy a book.

We moved to Brooklyn at the end of August, just in time to get me enrolled in a new school. Belle was in the RD class, the second-half of the freshman year of high school. She did not transfer, however, and continued to travel to P.S. 12 on the East Side. Jackson Street was a very long walk from the Delancey Street station.

I was to enter the seventh grade. I did not make the rapid class at first, because I had skipped a sixth-grade class. It became Mama's job to get me in school. Ordinarily, you get admitted into a school with transfer records. Not so with me. We went to a junior high school, P.S. 149, about nine blocks from our house. We were told we were out of the district. We ended up going from school to school, and they kept saying we were out of the district. Finally, they allowed me to enroll in P.S. 149.

The nine-block distance did not faze Mama. Whenever it rained after the school day had started, Mama would bring me boots and an umbrella. There were many days that I forgot my lunch. Mama would invariably bring it to me.

Mama made the most delicious *pirishkes* for Rosh Hashanah. When we were all living at home and younger, it was no problem. But when we got married and were scattered, it was not so easy for Mama. She saved tin boxes and did the baking in South Fallsburg. When Belle and Allan left New York, she shipped them. Even when she was already ailing, she lovingly made and shipped the *pirishkes*.

MEMORIES

By A. Allan Finkel

Dear Nieces and Nephews,

At Murray's urging, I have agreed to put into words some stories, incidents, and miscellany as pertains to us as we were growing up. To better understand this nostalgic trip down memory lane, it is important that you comprehend the times and circumstances.

Without going into specifics, both Grandpa and Grandma arrived in the United States in 1905, after having fled the tyrannies, anti-Semitism, persecutions, poverty, and hunger of Eastern Europe. Grandpa was twenty-years old at the time and, like thousands of others, was a deserter from the Tsarist Russian Army. He took up the trade of carpentry as his father before him. Grandma was fifteen-years old and had seen the horrors of a pogrom which had killed her mother. She was unhappy with her stepmother and lonely for her older sister, who was already in the United States.

Grandpa and Grandma settled in the Lower East Side of New York, met each other, and married in 1910. They had simply moved from one *shtetel* to another. Yiddish was the primary language spoken at home by the entire family. By the time Murray was born in 1922, Belle was twelve, Esther was nine, and I was five-years old. We had been exposed to English, which became our second language.

As we were growing up, there was no television, no refrigerator (we had an icebox until about 1939), and no radio until about the same time. When we got our first radio, Grandpa made one provision—it had to be a radio that carried a "Jewish Hour." Many of the things the present generation takes for granted were not even in existence. For example, who heard of air conditioning? In the summer we sweltered.

I recall Grandpa making a loan from the New Lots Credit Union (later "Beneficial Union") and on Thursday nights, if Grandma said I was a good boy, I would accompany Grandpa, and he would let me make the fifty-cent weekly payment.

We never went on a vacation, except for one summer when we went to the "country" for two weeks at the Shady Hill House in Hunter, New York, because Esther was so sickly. I can recall only one time as a child that we went on a picnic to Prospect Park. On another occasion we went to Coney Island. I was pleasantly surprised how well Grandpa could swim.

Life revolved around family and synagogue. Grandpa was already out of the house when we woke up and still busy at something when we went to bed. Grandma was constantly cooking, cleaning, and taking care of us.

Each of us had a special designation. Belle was the oldest; Esther was the youngest girl; I was the oldest son; Murray was the youngest. Each designation indicated a special degree of importance.

I recall a conversation at Grandpa and Grandma's fiftieth anniversary party in 1960 at Murray's house in Franklin Square. Someone asked Esther as to where I fitted in. When she replied that I was the third one, I looked in surprise. I was forty-three-years old at the time, and it was the first time in my life that I was something other than the "oldest boy."

On Saturdays we would do our visiting, either to the Bronx to Aunt Dora and Uncle Bernie's, or to Uncle Julius and Tante Rivke Rachel's. Invariably when boarding the train (Pennsylvania Avenue Station of the IRT, 7th Avenue New Lots Line), Grandma (with a bag of rags in a shopping bag) and Esther would stand at the rear of the car while the rest of us took seats. It seems that Esther had a chronically squeamish stomach and would become violently sick once the train started moving. It was not until she vomited and Grandma wiped it up with the rags that she had brought along, hopefully before we changed trains at Utica Ave., that they would join us.

On alternate Saturdays we would shlepp with two trolleys to Borough Park to visit Uncle Harry and Aunt Esther. On the Saturdays that we didn't go visiting, the locals—the Kobrins, the Charlie Finkels, the Abe Finkels plus Clara and Abram Rubin, and the Sroil Rubins—would gather at our house. Uncle Morris and Tante Bronche lived in Carnegie, Pennsylvania for awhile and then moved to Brooklyn and lived at 1013 Dumont Avenue.

I attended Hebrew School five days a week, Monday through Thursday and Sunday. On weekdays, I went from 4 to 6 p.m. in the lower grades and from 6 to 8 p.m. in the higher grades. Sunday classes were from 9 to 11 a.m. On Friday nights and Saturday mornings, I attended religious services. There were no other priorities; attending services was as natural as breathing.

The only toys I ever had was a sled, a Flexible Flyer that Grandpa picked up second-hand, and when I became a little older, a pair of Union Hardware roller skates that cost $1.49.

Twice per year, before Rosh Hashanna and before Pesach, Grandma would take me to Levinson's on Stone Avenue and Belmont for my fall and spring wardrobes. Each comprised of a suit with two pairs of pants that cost seven dollars for the ensemble. One pair of pants was to be worn daily; the jacket and other pair of trousers were reserved for the Sabbath, Holidays, and other festive occasions. The suit bought at Passover was to last until Rosh Hashanna. The suit bought in the fall was to last until Passover. Of course nothing ever fit me at the time of purchase, since Grandma always bought a suit that was a size larger so that I "would grow into it." By the time I "grew into it," it was already worn and ready for the trash can.

I was entitled to a pair of shoes with each suit, normally purchased at Thom McAnn at $3.35 per pair. I was also allotted one pair of sneakers, which was purchased for $1.49 in time for the summer recess. They could only be worn, according to Grandma's personal calendar, between July 1ˢᵗ and Labor Day. There were just two seasons: summer and winter. Summer began July 1ˢᵗ and lasted until Labor Day, which coincided with the beginning of winter. If the sneakers wore out before Labor Day, and they usually did, you simply stuck a piece of cardboard inside the sole. Even if the thermometer read 100 degrees on Labor Day, out came the one-piece union suit. I didn't have the nerve, but I recall that Murray, in a fit of rage, lopped off the sleeves and legs of his union suit.

I don't believe that Grandpa ever earned as much as five dollars per hour, and he was considered a skilled carpenter. Of course, a dollar went much further in those days. Subway and bus fare were five cents; admission to movies was ten cents. In 1938, when I graduated from NYU, I bought a 1935 Dodge for $250. Gasoline was twenty cents per gallon. I was dating Aunt Adele at the time. If we went to a downtown Brooklyn movie on a Saturday night—Paramount, Fox, RKO, or Albee (the Albee included Vaudeville)—the admission price was fifty cents and included a double feature. Then we went to either The Chocolate Shop on Pitkin Avenue or Meyers on Flatbush Avenue for a BLT and a chocolate malted for fifty cents. A total expenditure for the evening could run as high as $2.75.

If anybody in the family moved, the first question asked was, "Near what subway station?" Living near a subway station was better than living near a bus stop, because the latter meant an additional fare if you were going into the city.

If we were poor I wasn't aware of it. We had plenty to eat, the house was warm in the wintertime, and we had warm clothing to wear. But most of all, we had two wonderful parents who wanted something better out of life for their children than they had. Grandpa wanted his children to earn a living with "their heads not their hands." The hands tire with the years whereas the brain ages and matures with the years. Unequivocally, my growing-up years were the happiest years of my life, and I wouldn't trade them for anything in the world. We were very rich!

We were still living on the Lower East Side. Esther, who was about eight-years old, came home from school and advised Grandma that she was transferred to a school a considerable distance from our home. Grandma quickly ran to the school and cornered the principal. He advised her that the matter was no longer in his domain and that the school superintendent had made the decision.

The next morning, with me in tow and pregnant with Murray, Grandma trekked down to the superintendent's office. She was quickly advised that the superintendent saw no one without an appointment. Grandma asked the secretary if the superintendent made an appointment to go to the bathroom. She said that she was sure he did not. Grandma replied, "Tell him to make believe that he has to go to the bathroom again." With this, Grandma sat down and advised the secretary that she would just sit and wait. There was no way that that man was going to get out of his office and not see Grandma. All this started early in the morning. It was almost "quitting time" when the secretary told Grandma, "He will see you now." Ushered into the superintendent's office, Grandma told him of the purpose of her visit. When she was through, the superintendent said that he could not transfer just one child back to the school. What about the other children in the class? Grandma simply said, "So transfer all of them back." He did.

I vividly recall Saturday mornings, especially when I was eight- or nine-years old and Murray was three or four. The pace was much slower and relaxed. We were usually invited into Grandma and Grandpa's bedroom. Murray would get into bed with Grandma, and I would join Grandpa. Grandma would joke with us and tell us stories. If we coaxed her, she would sing her favorite song, "Rozinkes Und Mandlin" ("Raisins and Almonds"). After a while, she would say, "Tseit Tsu Gein in Shul. (Time to get ready to go to the synagogue.)" After I donned my Sabbath suit, I would sit down at the kitchen table, and Grandma would cut a thick piece of challah that she had baked the previous day. She would thickly smear it with *schmaltz*, and I would voraciously eat it with a glass of hot tea. Then Grandpa and I would leave for Shul.

When we reached the street, Grandpa turned to the left to attend services with his father at the Shul on Malta Street. I turned to the right to attend services at the Junior Congregation of the New Lots Talmud Torah. When the services were over, Grandpa was always waiting for me, and we would walk home together.

In her prime, I would match Grandma's culinary talents with anyone's. If Grandma had prepared a *cholent* (taken from the French *chaud lent*—to warm slowly), I was in heaven. In her prime, her *cholent* was absolutely the finest food I ever ate. I recall seeing Abram Rubin (Grandma's nephew) one Saturday with one foot on the chair on which he rested the iron pot, so that he could better scrape it to the last delicious drop. On other occasions, she made a *merrin* (carrots) *tsimmis*. It was also delicious. Her stuffed breast of veal, *kishka*, stuffed *helzel*, *teigarts* (a thick, greasy, but mouth-watering potato pancake), eggs fried in chicken fat, *retach* and *schmaltz* (chopped radishes, onions, and chicken fat), homemade barley and mushroom soup, and so many other dishes too numerous to mention, put her in a culinary class by herself. Watching her chop noodles was a site to behold.

On the baking side, nothing could match her *lekach* (honey cake), sponge cake topped with strawberries and real whipped cream, her *madel breit, putter kichel* (a cinnamon danish that we dipped in sour cream), her *piroshkes* which she made for Rosh Hashannah, and I can go on and on . . .

Grandma was a firm believer in old-world remedies. Her children were her victims. There is no counting the mustard plasters that she used on us. To avoid catching polio (this was long before the Salk vaccine), we wore camphor bags around our necks. When we had a chest cold, then known as "the grippe," Grandma would rely on a professional *banke shteller* (a method of leeching). A cup was used to draw the blood to the surface of the body by forming a vacuum over the spot believed to be the source of infection.

After Ethel, Charlie, and Abe married, the apartment above ours became vacant. One of the tenants was the Ginchansky family. Grandpa came home one evening and was told the disturbing news that the Ginchanskys were moving. When Grandpa said "So we will get another tenant," Grandma's response was "Will it be someone who could *shtell bankes* like Mrs. Ginchansky?"

It was Kol Nidre night, 1922. We had just returned from services. "We" included Grandpa; Grandma, who was pregnant with Murray; Belle; Esther; and me. We were living on the fourth floor of a cold-water tenement on the Lower East Side. I insisted that Grandma carry me up the stairs. It was not but a few hours later that Grandpa woke us up to tell us that we had a new brother. Since Succoth was approaching, Grandpa built a succah on the roof in which the bris was to take place. Grandma was up and around in a few days, baking and cooking for the big event. The morning of the bris, Grandpa said to Grandma, "Es Pazt Nischt, Gei Zurich In Bet." A liberal translation would be, "In your delicate condition, it would not look right to be up and around. Why don't you get back in bed?"

It was January 10, 1927, the day your Great Grandmother Pearl died. I was nine-years old at the time. As the family was getting ready to leave for the funeral, Grandma turned to me and said that there was no need for me to join them, that I would have enough dealings with death when I grew older. My first question was "Do I have to go to Hebrew School?" to which Grandma responded, "Fardrey Zich Dein Kup Und Tu Vos Du Vilst. (Don't bother me, do what you want to do.)" I decided right then and there that I would not go to Hebrew School.

The next day the Hebrew teacher asked me (conversation was always in Yiddish) the reason for my absence the day before. When I advised him that, "Die Bube Hut Geshtorben (My grandmother died)," his quick response was, "Hust Du Gegangen Tsu De Levaye? (Did you go to the funeral?)" When I foolishly told him the truth, that I did not go, he said that in that case I should have come to Hebrew School. The session was from 4 to 6. When I was getting ready to leave, he turned to me and said (in Yiddish), "You are staying until 8 p.m. I have already spoken to your mother, and she notified me that you have already done your homework and that she will keep your supper warm for you." When I queried him as to why he was punishing me because my grandmother died, his response was, "I am not punishing you, but your father paid hard-earned money to send you to Hebrew School, and I want to make sure that he gets his money's worth." Tuition at the time was two dollars per month. At twenty sessions, this averaged out to ten cents per session.

Portions of the next short talk may have two versions. One is mine, the accurate one. The other is Murray's. Murray was only eight-years old at the time. What he does not remember he tends to fabricate.

It was the Friday of my Bar Mitzvah. I was already in Thomas Jefferson High School's annex at P.S. 150 at Christopher and Blake. I went to the early session, from 7 a.m. to 1 p.m., so I was home by 2 p.m. Murray was going to P.S. 190 (just across from our home), and he did not get out until 3 p.m. It was wintertime, and we played hockey on roller skates. Murray accused me of stealing his hockey puck, and we began pushing and shoving each other. A friend of mine, Davy Stern, intervened and told me to stop picking on a little kid and to pick on somebody my own size. Before long, he and I began punching each other until I ended up with a black eye that was a lulu. Just as this altercation was about to conclude, Murray threw the puck at me. He caught me in the middle of my forehead, which swelled immediately. So I attended my Bar Mitzvah with one eye closed and a large *bile* on my forehead.

Grandma had a soft heart for those less fortunate than her. She had met a Mrs. Fishman in the chicken market. Mrs. Fishman was a widow who owned a small dairy, which she operated with her son. After bewailing her sad fate, she evoked a promise from Grandma to buy milk from her. I was assigned the daily chore of going for a pitcher of milk from Fishman's Dairy.

One summer afternoon, Grandma called out to me "Tseit Tsu Gein Far Milch. (Time to go for milk.)" Since I was in the middle of a punchball game, I yelled back, "Ich Hab Nischt Kein Tseit. (I don't have time.)" After awhile I said to myself, "That's no way to talk to Mama," so I rang the bell, and when Grandma answered, I said, "Ich Vel Gein Yetst. (I'll go now.)" To which Grandma responded, "Yetst Darf Ich Nischt De Milch, Uber Ven Der Tate Kumt Aheim Vel Ich Im Zagen Az Du Hust Nischt Gevalt Gein Far De Milch Un Du Vest Chappen Klep. (When Papa comes home I'll tell him that you refused to go for milk, and I'm sure you will get a beating.)" Though Grandpa never raised a hand at any of us, I pleaded with Grandma, "Ich Vil Gein, Ich Vil Gein. Zug Nischt Der Taten. (I'll go, I'll go. Please don't tell Papa.)" She grudgingly acquiesced, gave me the money for the milk, and never, to my knowledge, reported the incident to Grandpa.

My allowance was two cents per day, which I had already received and spent in the morning. It was a hot summer day, and after lunch I asked Grandma for three cents for an ice cream cone. I yelled and carried on until Grandma opened her change purse, took out three pennies, and threw them at me, saying "Luz Mir Shein Alaine. (Leave me alone already.)" I quickly ran to Cheap Izzy's and bought the delicious delicacy of a scoop of chocolate ice cream in a sugar cone covered with chocolate sprinkles.

That evening, as it was customary in the summertime, Grandpa took out the folding chairs, and he and Grandma would sit outside the house. At about 9 p.m., Grandpa would say "Lum Mir Gein Far A Shpatsir. (Let's take a walk.)" Grandma would take Murray's hand, and I would walk alongside Grandpa. We would walk to New Lots and Sheffield, turn back, and then head for home with a stop at Cheap Izzy's to buy ice cream cones for Murray and me. This particular evening, just as Grandpa was about to place his order for two cones, Grandma pointed to me and said, "Er Hut Shein Gehat Zeins. (He already had his.)" Grandpa ordered one cone and gave it to Murray. I didn't utter a sound. Grandma was just being fair. I already had mine.

Grandpa came home from work one day, looked at Grandma, and said, "Du Kukst A Bissel Fartracht. Vos Iz Der Mer? (You look a little disturbed. What's the matter?)" Grandma responded, "Ich Denk Az Ich Hab Kekeift A Tschicken Mit A Makke. (I think the chicken I bought has a blemish.)" Grandpa suggested that Grandma take the chicken and show it to the Rabbi to check if it was kosher. The next morning Grandma put the chicken in a shopping bag and took it to the synagogue to show the Rabbi.

When Grandpa came home that evening, he asked, "Vos Hut Passirt? (What happened?)" Grandma's response was, "Ich Vel Keinmul Gein Zurick Tsu Im. (I'll never go back to him.) Ich Hab Im Gevizen Die Makke, Und Er Kukt Mir Gleich In Eig Arain Und Frekt Mir, (I showed him the blemish, he looked at me straight in the eye and asks,) 'Eyer Man Arbet? Er Macht A Leben? Die Kinder Habben Genug Tsu Essen? In hoiz Iz Varen? Ihr Kent Gatzulin Die Rent? (Is your husband working? Does he make a living? Do the children have enough to eat? Is the house warm in the winter? Can you pay the rent?) Eib Der entfer is Avade, Gib Die Tshicken Zu An Arum Und Keift An Ander. (If the answer is yes to all my questions, give the chicken to a poor person and then buy another for yourself.)'"

"Vus Hus Du Getun? (What did you do?)" Grandpa queried. Grandma replied, "Ich Hab Aroisgeshnitten Die Makke. (I cut off the blemish and we will have the chicken for supper.)"

I was about five-years old at the time. We were living on the Lower East Side within the shadows of the Williamsburg Bridge. On Sunday morning, when the weather was nice, Grandpa would take me with him as he would visit relatives and *lansleit* (people whose origins were the same as his). I particularly relished visiting one particular "landsman" who I considered to be a magician, although he actually was a harness maker. He had a dark, dingy, dreary shop that had a sharp odor of tanned leather about it. While he worked, he would hold a conversation with Grandpa. I sat in awe and watched his magic. Every so often he would thread a needle with white thread and run his fingers over the thread, which would instantly turn black.

Time after time, I would come home and ask Grandma to thread a needle for me. I would then run my fingers over the thread, but the thread never changed colors. I would constantly ask Grandpa to take me back to the shop. There just had to be something I overlooked. What I had overlooked was that the landsman's hands were greasy when he ran his fingers over the thread.

One Sunday, as Grandpa and I were returning home through the crowded streets, we heard someone shouting, "Help, help, thief, robber!" Grandpa spied the thief, gave chase, caught him, and held him down until the police came.

Grandpa was excited! He triumphantly came home and yelled out at Grandma, "Gechapt A Goniff! (I caught a thief!)" Grandma, who was pregnant at the time with Murray, yelled back, "In Drerd Mit Dem Goniff, Avu Iz Mein Zun? (To hell with the thief, where's my son?)"

In the meantime, I had been left standing alone. A crowd gathered including a burly Irish cop who kept asking me a lot of questions. I, on the other hand, spoke only Yiddish and did not understand a word he said to me. But I was not concerned, because Grandma prepared me for a moment like this: "Az Du Vest Farloren Veren, Red Tsu Keinem.

Ich Vel Dir Gefinen. (If you ever get lost, speak to no one. I will find you.)" I knew that Grandma would keep her promise.

At long last, both Grandma and Grandpa breathlessly and with sighs of relief appeared and rescued me from the crowd.

We were living on New Lots Avenue in Brooklyn. I was in second grade at P.S. 190. My teacher's name was Mrs. Sacks. It was the next to last day of Open School Week, when the school opened for visitors. Mrs. Sacks took me aside and asked me why my mother had not visited the class. Frankly, I was embarrassed because I had never heard Grandma speak English. Pressured by Mrs. Sacks, I asked Grandma if she had any intentions of coming to school. Her answer was, "Ich Hab Gevart Far Dir Tsu Fregen. (I was waiting for you to invite me.)"

The next morning there was a knock on the classroom door and a beautiful lady came in, very nicely dressed, and began a very animated conversation in English with the teacher. Occasionally they turned to me and laughed while I sat in amazement. It was Grandma speaking English, something I had never heard her do before.

When I came home and said that I didn't know that she could speak English, her response was simple. She knew that my primary language would be English, but she spoke Yiddish so that Yiddish would not be foreign to me.

For the High Holy Days, we always attended services at your Great Grandfather's shul. Year after year, we sat in the same row that began with 330, purposely selected because we lived at 330 New Lots Avenue. The seating, starting with the window, was occupied by your Great Grandfather, myself, Grandpa, Murray, Uncle Charlie, Uncle Sam, Uncle Abe, and on Yom Kippur, we would squeeze in Uncle Bernie.

I was at the age when I asked a lot of questions. Grandpa's most popular response was "Azei Iz Dus Geshriben. (It is so written.)" If I asked too many questions, he would say "Shein Genug Mit Frages. (Enough already with the questions.)"

It was Yom Kippur, and we had reached the *Birkas Kohanim* (blessing of the priests) portion of the service. I noticed that most of the congregants covered their heads and faces with their prayer shawls, and quite a number, including Grandpa, turned and faced the rear of the sanctuary. The ritual that followed was one that was prescribed in the Bible. The Levites washed the feet of the *Kohanim,* and then the High Priest would enter the "Holy of Holies," a site so awesome that it was forbidden to look at them. But this explanation had not been made to me! So when I asked Grandpa as to what was going on, his response was, "Men Tor Nischt Kukin. (It is forbidden to look.)" I then asked him what would happen if I just took a little peek. His response was, "Du Vest Veren Bleend Af Ein Eig. (You will be blind in one eye.)" I then asked him what would happen if I took a second peek. His response was, "Du Vest Veren Bleend Af Beide Eigen. (You'll become blind in both eyes.)" I asked my final question as to what would happen if I looked a third time. His quick response was, "Ich Vel Dir Geben A Frask Uber Dem Panim. (I'll smack you across the face.)"

From the ages of nine to fifteen, I sang in a choir for the High Holy Days. This one year, I was in a choir conducted by Willie Secunda, the brother of the well-known Jewish composer and lyricist, Sholom Secunda. (One of his more popular songs was "Bei Mir Bist Du Schoen.") We were singing at the Pennsylvania Avenue Synagogue at Pennsylvania and New Lots. Cantor Nisselson had a beautiful voice. His contract called for him to also do the Succoth service, but he became ill and could not perform. Our choir leader was also an actor's agent and a wheeler dealer. He told us that the great cantor Yosele Rosenblatt owed him a favor, and he convinced him to conduct the service. After the service on the first day of Succoth, Grandpa came down to the choir room and waited for me to take off my robe and get into my street clothes so we could walk home. Cantor Rosenblatt spied Grandpa and asked him what he was doing in the choir room. Grandpa responded, "Ich Vart Fra Mein Zun. (I'm waiting for my son.)" Cantor Rosenblatt then asked Grandpa, "Vee Hut Ihr Geglichen Mein Davenen? (How did you like my service?)" Grandpa, who always spoke his mind, responded, "Ihr Hut Zich Nischt Ubergearbet. (You really did not knock yourself out.)" Cantor Rosenblatt looked at Grandpa and said, "Kumt Tsurick Morgen. (Come back tomorrow.)"

The next day, when Grandpa came to the choir room after services, Cantor Rosenblatt repeated the previous day's question. The response from Grandpa was, "Heint Hut Ihr Gedavent!" Literally translated, "Today you really did a job!"

Belle graduated from Maxwell Training School for Teachers. Grandpa was ecstatic. Not only was his daughter the first Finkel to graduate from college, she also had a profession. She was the epitome of Grandpa's wish—that his children would earn a living with their brains, not their hands. When she passed her teaching exams and received her teaching license, he was truly proud. But then the sad realities began. It was 1932, the height of the Depression, and the New York city school system was not making regular appointments. Belle would get up at the crack of dawn and make the rounds of the schools seeking a day's work as a substitute, but to no avail.

It was February 1940. Grandma and Grandpa celebrated their thirtieth wedding anniversary by taking a trip to Cleveland, Ohio, to visit Grandma's sister, Tante Deveira. I was already dating Aunt Adele and decided that it was time for her to meet my parents. Aunt Adele and I went in my 1935 Dodge to Grand Central Station to pick them up. After the introductions, we drove home. We sat around the kitchen table, noshed, and talked. At about 11 p.m. or so, I drove Adele to her home. (She lived on Legion Street near the Saratoga Ave. station of the IRT.)

When I came home, Grandpa was waiting up for me. I had no sooner entered the apartment when I noticed a great big smile on Grandpa's face. He said, "Ich Gleich Ihr. (I liked her.)" My first question was, "Farvos Gleichst Du Ihr? (Why do you like her?)" His response was, "Zie Trukt Nisht Kein Negel Polish. (She doesn't wear any nail polish.)" At this point I could not contain myself. Earlier in the evening, when I had picked Adele up, she apologized for not wearing nail polish. Adele was a science major at Brooklyn College, and the formaldehyde in the science lab removed the nail polish.

Tender Memories of My Zeyde

By A. Allan Finkel

To those of you who were born after 1945, you missed the great pleasure of knowing your great grandfather (or great great grandfather) Aryeh Leib (Louis) Finkel. He was a kind and gentle man, and I never heard him chastise anyone.

He and I were very close. In 1923, we were already living on New Lots Avenue. Zeyde, your great grandmother Pearl, and the then unmarried children, Charlie, Ethel, and Abe, had the upstairs apartment. Mom has just enrolled me in elementary school. (I was five-years old.) When Zeyde was advised of this important news, he turned to Mom and said, "Az er iz alt genug tsu gein in skul iz alt genug tsu gein in cheder. (If he is old enough to go to school, he's old enough to go to Hebrew school.)"

Without further ado, he took me by the hand, and we walked the two blocks to the New Lots Talmud Torah and registered me there. We then went to the bookstore down the street, and he bought two books for me, a *Raishes Das* (a beginner's book) and a *Siddur*. He then took a package of lifesavers from his pocket, handed it to me and said, "May your Hebrew studies be as sweet and enjoyable as this package of candy."

Zeyde was born in 1864, during the height of the Victorian era. This dictated his style of clothes. He always wore a "Prince Albert" (a type of jacket that was worn by Prince Albert, Queen Victoria's consort), a derby, and on the Sabbath and Holidays, he wore striped pants. His beard was snow white, and he always had a clean, refreshing scent about him.

I recall one incident when he was dressing prior to going to the Synagogue one Sabbath. Uncle Abe suggested that he should put on a certain tie that he gave Great Grandpa. Zeyde commented that the tie had a stain. When Uncle Abe said that the beard would cover the stain, his reply was that, "the stain would still be there, and I know it."

For the High Holy Days, Pop, Uncle Sam, Uncle Charlie, and Uncle Abe joined Zeyde in his Shul on Malta Street. We had a whole row for the family.

My brother Murray was born on Yom Kippur. As a birthday present, Zeyde bought the honor of *Gelila,* tying the Torah before returning it to the Ark. In those days they auctioned off the honors. No one would dare bid against Zeyde because of the great respect they all showed for him. Murray had the honor of *Gelila* from the age of thirteen to twenty-one, the year he went into the army.

The day after Yom Kippur meant that it was time to get ready for Succoth. Every year, a Sukkah was constructed in the backyard. On its completion, Great Grandpa would rent a pushcart for five cents per day, and he and I would head for Canarsie, where we would pull up sea reeds (*Schach*) to be used as the Sukkah's roof. The entire family would eat in the Sukkah during the first and last days of the eight-day holiday. Zeyde, however, would eat all his meals there, even in inclement weather. Grandpa permitted me to eat with him when the weather was nice.

On the lighter side, I recall the preparation for Sam and Goldie Finkel's wedding, August 1933. Zeyde asked me to go to the hardware store and get a "specific hydrometer." When I placed my order, the hardware store owner said to me, "I guess your grandfather is making some bootleg whiskey." When I gave him the hydrometer, he went into the bathroom and checked the brew that was in the bathtub. He then filled about a hundred pint bottles. Half were labeled "Three Feathers," the other half "Golden Wedding," two well-known brands of rye. There were distributed at the wedding. Zeyde then made a survey, questioning everybody, "Velecha gefelt aich besser? (Which is better?)" Of course he did not tell them that both were from the same batch of bootleg liquor.

⟋

Most of the family lived within walking distance of Zeyde. Grandpa would usually alternate visiting our family and Uncle Abe's after the morning service and Uncle Sam's and Uncle Charlie's families after the evening service. He would alternate his visits so he could see all the children and adults at least every other day. When Zeyde walked up the stairs, he purposely made lots of noise so he could allow Murray and me time to get our yarmulkes. We would never allow Grandpa to catch us without our skull caps. If Zeyde missed a day visiting, someone would be sent to check out the reason why. Grandpa did not have a telephone.

⟋

I am sure that you are aware that a dead person's body is very rarely brought into a sanctuary, because it would make a sanctuary unclean. The members of Zeyde's congregation thought so highly of him that they brought his body into the sanctuary. Such an honor is reserved for *Tsadikim*, saintly people, which meant that the sanctuary had to be cleaned from top to bottom.

STORIES AND ANECDOTES OF MY FATHER

By Murray I. Finkel

he Red Baseball Bat

I had the only red baseball bat in the neighborhood. Before Pesach, Pop would buy bushel baskets of grapes and make his own Passover wine. He would squash the grapes with my baseball bat, and when the grapes were converted into liquid form, Pop would stir the wine with the baseball bat. After a few years of this annual procedure, my bat was a dark, winy red.

Kearney Ship Yard

During the war, Pop was working in the Kearney New Jersey Ship Yards constructing pontoon bridges. Pop was warned continuously by the other workers that he was working too fast and producing too much. Since Pop had two sons in combat overseas, he disregarded the warning. Pop came home from work one day with his face all bruised and swollen and his body full of welts from the beating he took from his coworkers.

Carpentry Work in Forest Hills

Our cousins Murray and Rhoda purchased a home in Forest Hills. They were anxious to move in but were being held up by uncompleted alterations and renovations. They asked Pop if he could help the contractor complete some built-in cabinets. Pop, a skilled carpenter, was working part-time in those years and therefore was available. Dotty was to drive Pop to Forest Hills, and Rhoda was to drive him home to Brooklyn.

Dotty received a call from Pop in the early afternoon of the first day Pop was on the job. Pop asked Dotty to please pick him up and take him home. After inquiring what happened, Pop said, "Alle Halbe shtunde hut er gezucht, 'Mr. Finkel, vash di hent.' Hub ich geentfert, 'vus bin ich, a carpenter tzei a surgeon?' (Every half hour he said, 'Mr. Finkel, wash your hands.' [Pop kept getting his fingerprints on the wood.] I answered, 'What am I, a surgeon or a carpenter?' So I quit.)"

Additions to Our House in Franklin Square

When we purchased our home in Franklin Square, we would take Pop along with us during our periodic inspections to review the work in process. On this particular Sunday, after picking up Mom and Pop in Brooklyn for our weekly visit to check on the progress of our new house, Pop said that he would meet us by the car. After stopping off in his cellar, Pop arrived carrying a shovel and a pickle barrel with the top and bottom removed. After inquiring about the purpose of the barrel, Pop said he would explain later.

Pop led me down to the area of the intended laundry room. The cellar floor was not cemented as yet. He dug a hole, placed the pickle barrel in the ground, and covered the opening with a drain. We had the only laundry room with a drain in the development. It sure came in handy the few times we had trouble with the washing machine and plumbing.

Our house was a basic ranch, and we always intended to eventually add an attached garage, closed porch, and finished basement. Pop was semi-retired at the time and could hardly wait to start on the additions.

Pop's favorite construction task was mixing cement. When we discussed the foundation and floors for the garage and porch, Pop insisted on mixing the cement by hand. I said, "No way." I was holding out for ready-mixed poured cement from a truck. We finally compromised on renting a Sear's home cement mixer. I also bought Pop a circular power saw. He had only used hand tools throughout his carpentry career. Pop would keep the power saw on one side of the garage and the handsaw on the other. He used whichever one was closer.

I planned my vacation so I could help Pop with the heavy work, such as mixing the cement and putting in the foundation. But Pop was a professional and very intolerant towards amateurs when it came to construction. I would be holding a ladder for Pop and he would point to a pile of tools and say, "Give me that one." When I gave him the wrong one, which invariably occurred, he said I should have known which tool he needed. Pretty soon my job was limited to cleaning up after Pop and purchasing the materials.

The closed porch was a continuation of the garage. When Pop was building the combined roof, he would rest the long crossbeams on a T-bar. Mom would hold the bar in place, and Pop would bang in the nails. They would then repeat the procedure on the other side of the house.

While Pop was building the garage and porch, three young fellows were constructing a detached garage across the street. They were amazed at Pop's speed and innovations. In fact, he completed all our outside additions before they finished the garage.

Eventually, Pop finished the basement and converted the porch into a den with heat and air conditioning. Years later, when the boys were in college and Shelley was living in Queens, Pop came to me with a proposition. He wanted to build another extension to the house. This time, he would go up and build two additional bedrooms and a bathroom. Pop (who was over eighty at the time), Uncle Harry, and Uncle Charlie would start Saturday night after sundown. He guaranteed to have the new addition framed out by Monday. I said, "Pop, Shelley has her own apartment, and the boys will likely find their own places to live after they finish college, so we don't need the additional bedrooms." Pop answered, "But my brothers owe me time." It seems that Pop and his brothers never paid each other for their work but kept a record of their time helping each other.

Pop and the Pea Soup

Every year in late September or early October, Pop, Albert, and I would make our last trip of the year to South Fallsburg to winterize and close the bungalow for the season. This particular morning, the weather was extremely cold for so early in the fall, so I mentioned to Pop and Albert that it would be a good idea to stop off at the town diner for some hot soup before we continued on to the bungalow.

After checking the menu for the soup that I thought would be safe from non-kosher ingredients, I selected pea soup. Pop's hands were like leather from being an old-time carpenter, and he had a throat lining to match from drinking hot tea in a glass all his life. Before I had a chance to swallow one tablespoon of soup, Pop was halfway through his bowl. Much to my dismay, I discovered pieces of ham in the bowl. Being in a dilemma whether to tell Pop or not, I remembered that Pop was hard of hearing. I therefore whispered, "Ich daink aas er is a pur shticklach chaser in der zoop. (I think there are a few pieces of ham in the soup.)" Pop did not say a word but continued eating his soup. As we left the diner, Pop looked around and said to me, "Du deinkst aas de Ruv hut mir gezen? (Do you think the Rabbi saw me?)"

Kiddish in Honor of Pop's 90th Birthday

In honor of Pop's 90th birthday, we sponsored a sit-down kiddish at the Oakland Jewish Center in Bayside. Pop's children, grandchildren, brothers and sisters, and nieces and nephews were all present. My brother

Allan had a beautiful voice, and there was nothing that my father enjoyed more than to hear my brother preside as the cantor at the Temple service. Allan was the cantor at the kiddish, but unfortunately Pop was practically deaf and did not hear a word of my brother's singing.

After the service was over, everyone congratulated Pop on his birthday and on the beautiful job Allan did on his *dovening* as a cantor. Pop said, "Ich hub nit gehert a vort, ubber ich hub geshept noches vile ich gedenk ozz yurn, tzueik hubich goot gehert zine shtime. (I didn't hear a word, but I'm still very proud, because I can still remember his voice from years back.)"

Tarring the Bungalow Roof

On one of my frequent visits to Pop in Bayside, he asked me to drive him to South Fallsburg so he could repair the roof on the bungalow. I asked, "Wouldn't it be more feasible to hire a professional roofer to do the job?" Pop disagreed, saying that they did not do a good enough job. I told Pop that at ninety-years old, he was too old to do tarring, and that I would hire a roofer. He then said that he would take the bus and go up by himself. Naturally, I thought he was kidding.

Esther called the next day saying that Viola, who living above Pop, called and said that Pop went to South Fallsburg by bus. This meant that Pop took the city bus from Bayside to the subway, the subway to the bus terminal in Manhattan, and the bus to South Fallsburg. He then had to walk from the bus stop in town to the lumber yard and about two miles uphill to the house.

The next morning I drove my car to South Fallsburg. When I arrived, Pop was just about finished tarring the roof. I asked, "How did you get a hundred-pound can of tar up on the roof?" With a big smile, Pop answered, "I used pulleys, of course."

Renewal of the Lease

Whenever it was time to renew the lease on Pop's Bayside apartment, he gave us a hard time. The lease called for an increase of ten percent, and Pop remarked that he would offer management five percent. Rather than go through this periodic hassle with Pop, I called the office and asked them if they would please put the lease in my name. They were delighted to cooperate, because they remembered Pop from the last renewal. I warned them that Pop was coming in to offer them five percent and, if possible, to tell him that they were waiving the increase because he was over ninety-years old. Esther wrote the original rent check from Pop's checkbook and the additional ten percent increase on the other account where she had power of attorney. She enclosed both checks in an envelope, and Pop always personally delivered the envelope to the rental office.

The next morning, Dotty received a phone call from Esther saying that Pop was on the warpath. Pop did not sleep too well that night, and lying in bed he remembered that the envelope did not look just right. It seems that after Esther sealed the envelope, she did not remember if she signed the second check, so she opened the envelope and then resealed it with tape. When Pop opened the envelope and saw the two checks, he was fit to be tied.

We had Pop over for dinner, and he was still excited about the two checks. I asked him, "Pop, you own real estate with your brothers, and you're always getting increases. Why isn't your landlord entitled to the same increase?" His answer was, "We own rent-controlled property, and my building is not rent-controlled, therefore an increase of five percent is adequate." Then with a big smile, he said, "But you did not fool me. I found out about the increase on my own."

Pop and the Rabbi's Secretary

When Pop's Rabbi in Bayside had to make a Shivah visit, his secretary would call and ask Pop if he was available to come along. This was a great honor for Pop to have the Rabbi call. This was a common occurrence. Although Pop was hard of hearing, he was able to communicate with the secretary because she spoke in a low pitch.

Pop's lease was up for renewal, and he approached Esther saying, "Chopp nit mit der lease, ich hub a gedaynk. (Don't rush with the lease, I have an idea.)" He said that since the Rabbi's secretary was not married he had a proposition for her. He said that he would offer her $1,000 up-front money and $100 per month, and he would move in with her. Bearing in mind that the secretary was American-born, a college graduate, quite heavy, and only in her late fifties, Esther, with a straight face, answered, "Pop, do you realize that you're older than this girl's mother?" Pop responded, "Why, does she have a better offer?"

Pop and the Matzo Balls

We were visiting Pop in Bayside, and he was busy in the kitchen making matzo balls. I said, "Pop, where did you learn to make matzo balls?" He answered, "It's easy, the same ratio as mixing cement, three to one."

Pop's Nurse at Long Beach

When Pop was at the Senior Citizen Hotel at Long Beach, he would fall occasionally because of poor blood circulation to his head. While waiting for Pop to be admitted to the Hebrew Home in Riverdale, we hired a practical nurse to care for him. It so happened that the rather young nurse was in her first trimester of pregnancy and suffered from severe morning sickness that lasted most of the day. When we visited Pop, the nurse was usually the one resting in the bed, and Pop was catering to the nurse's needs. With a big smile, Pop would say, "Ich bin der tate foon der kinde. (I am the father of the baby.)"

Andy's Aufruf or Calling Up

On the Friday night before Sally and Andy's wedding, Andy's *Aufruf*, or "calling up," was to be celebrated at a very reform temple in Baltimore. The only ones in the synagogue wearing yarmulkes were Pop, Andy, Gary, and me.

The religious service was short, and instead of having the Rabbi's sermon, a Russian refugee, who the temple sponsored, performed a beautiful piano recital. After the recital, the mothers of the boys who were to be Bar Mitzvahed the following day lit the Friday night candles after sundown. They then took out the Torah, and the Bar Mitzvah boys and Andy received the blessings.

Pop was very orthodox and had never attended a reform service before. He was very tolerant of all the proceedings that transpired until they took the Torah out of the ark. He said, "Ich hub gezen allis, uber nit tzu oys nemen di torah freytich ba nacht. (I've seen everything, but never taking out the Torah on Friday night.)"

Sally and Andy's Wedding

Sally and Andy were married at the Suburban Country Club in Pikesville, Maryland. The affair was not kosher, so we ordered fish for Pop and some of the other relatives who so desired. Dotty and I were busy during the reception, so I put Allan in charge of Pop during the serving of the hors d'oeuvres. I warned my brother to keep a close eye on Pop because they were serving non-kosher food. As the waiter walked by with a tray of fish balls, Pop grabbed a handful, ate some, and said, "Takke dos is gutte white fish. (This is really good white fish.)" We never told him that he just consumed some crab balls.

Pop and the Hebrew School Window

I was playing box ball on the sidewalk of the Hebrew School with a few of the other students before the start of my Hebrew class. I accidentally broke a window and was caught in the act by Abe the custodian. He grabbed me by the back of the neck just as Pop was passing through on his way to visit his family on Vermont Street. Pop said, "Let go of my son." After being informed that I broke a window, he said "No problem, I'll fix it." He turned around, went home, and came back with a new windowpane, putty, etc., and replaced the broken window on the spot. I was saved a reprimand or punishment by the principal.

More Expansion Ideas

Pop completed the construction of the garage and den, and he was ready for the next project. We were sitting in our den and talking in generalities. Dotty remarked it would be nice to have a closet in the den so it could double as a guestroom. This plan was completely discarded because the room contained windows on two sides, the couch on the third side, and an outside door and television on the fourth. Next time we visited the folks, Pop said he had a surprise for us. He prefabricated the basic forms for a closet and wanted me to transport it in my car to Franklin Square. Since the den was directly behind the garage and the parking space for my car extended practically to the den wall, Pop was going to cut out an area in the wall above the height of the car hood. He was going to extend the closet into the garage and have it hang over the hood of the car. This meant that we would have to stand on a footstool to use this closet. The closet would be one-half the height of a normal one. Dotty vetoed the project.

Paneling the Boys Room

Pop originally paneled two of the four walls in the boys' room. Dotty asked Pop if he would mind paneling the remaining two walls. Pop was about eighty-seven-years old by then, but he still agreed to do the job. Andy and Gary's friends were astonished at how he managed to manipulate the large panels and fit them perfectly in their place. They were watching in amazement as he exhibited his carpentry skills, especially at his advanced age. They wouldn't leave until the job was completed.

Sid Shapiro's Basement

Pop loved communicating with Sid Shapiro, my next-door neighbor. Sid spoke Yiddish perfectly and had a very fine sense of humor. Sid was in the business of manufacturing fireproof doors, so he was familiar with carpentry. He had one or two of his employees finishing off his basement in their free time. They were slow and unreliable, and he asked

Pop if he would please complete the job. Pop agreed, and they discussed in detail the required work to be done. The next afternoon Sid called Pop and wanted some changes made to the agreed plans. Pop said, "I'm sorry but I already completed the basement."

Pop's Health

Dotty fell down the basement stairs in Franklin Square and fractured her coccyx and a few ribs. She was incapacitated in bed and was feeling a tremendous amount of pain. Pop was visiting and inquired, "Vus tust dew in bett? Dew bist a yunge madle. (What are you doing in bed? You are a young woman.)" Pop couldn't understand young people being sick. Pop's health was extremely good, and during his entire life he was laid up only twice. One week was for a hemorrhoid operation and the other was for prostate surgery. I don't remember Pop missing a day's work because of a cold or any respiratory illness.

Passover

Pop always conducted the Passover Seder. In his later years he would occasionally doze off for about ten or fifteen seconds at a time. We would observe patiently with the utmost respect and wait for Pop to resume the service. He would continue where he left off, never missing a word.

Pop's Dinners in Bayside

After Mom died, Pop made his own meals for a while. His favorite meal was *zup fleish*, soup meat, which he doled out with soup in an assembly line fashion in plastic containers. He froze the meat and soup and had enough for a week or two. He also had an old frying pan in which he prepared his eggs and cooked his other meals. The containers were not exactly clean and the outside of the pan was pitch black. Luckily, Pop had a cast iron stomach. The food in the refrigerator was mainly the leftovers from the Saturday kiddush at the temple. This consisted of herring, gefilte fish, various salads, cake, and cookies. Since

Pop was probably the oldest senior citizen attending the temple, they thought they were doing him a favor by loading him up with all the leftovers.

Dotty wasn't thrilled with Pop's diet, so she decided to prepare his meals. Dot would cook extra portions at our family meals and then package dinners for Pop in aluminum containers. They were balanced meals consisting of meat, fish, or chicken with potatoes, rice, or pasta, and a healthy vegetable. Pop would frequently join us for dinner and take home the prepared containers of food.

After a while, Pop stopped using the oven. I believe he became a little scared using the gas range. To heat the food he would remove the cover from his king-size tea kettle and place the food container over the opening and steam the food. This method was fine until we noticed that the kitchen towel, which was hanging on the door knob, was partially burned. Pop was probably removing the hot food container with the towel, and part of the towel was hanging over the gas flame on the stove. We then purchased a simple toaster oven and preset the dial. All Pop had to do was put in the plug to heat the food and pull it out after the dinner was heated.

Pop refused to use the oven. His new method of heating the food was to empty the contents into a pot, add some water, and cook the dinner on top of the stove. When we discovered Pop's latest method for heating the food, Dot added tomato sauce or tomato juice to all the dinners so Pop would not have to add water and the meals would be tastier.

Pop's Walk to Shul

After Mom died, Pop would go to services at the Shul morning and evening. He was Mister Reliable. Sun, rain, or snow, Pop would be there. A few of the boys in my office attended the same synagogue, and I would receive reports of Pop crossing Springfield Boulevard, a main thoroughfare. The horns were honking and the drivers yelling but Pop ignored everything and just continued to cross. I would dread phone calls between 5 and 7 p.m., hoping no one was calling to report an accident. God was looking after Pop.

Pop and the Rabbi

Pop was practically deaf but he was still able to participate in the prayers. At times he conducted services as the *Bar Tefillah*, the prayer reader. He knew the timing, so he was able to follow the *dovening*. The Rabbi would give him hand signals when it was his time to repeat the reader's portion of the prayers.

While we were sitting Shiva for Pop, Esther and I attended Sabbath services at Pop's synagogue. The Rabbi's complete sermon was a beautiful eulogy about Pop. We were proud.

GROWING UP IN BROOKLYN

By Murray I. Finkel

I was born on October 2, 1922, on Yom Kippur, at 285 Madison Street on the Lower East Side of Manhattan. My brother Allan was five; my sisters Esther and Belle were nine- and twelve-years old, respectively.

My bris took place in a Succah that Pop built on the roof of our tenement house. Even though Mom had just given birth, she did all the cooking and baking for the events that fell during the holiday of Succoth.

In 1923, Pop bought an attached house at 330 New Lots Avenue in the East New York section of Brooklyn. The building consisted of a store on the street level and six-room railroad-style apartments on the second and third floors. We rented the store and third-floor flat. There was a cellar that led to a small backyard. Pop built a Succah in the yard every Succoth holiday, and we ate our dinner meal there. Serving the meal was quite a job, because the only way into the backyard was up a steep staircase from the cellar, the old-fashioned type with the doors that open upward and lay flat on the ground when closed.

Since Allan and I were the youngest, we slept together in the middle room. We called it "Grand Central Station," because you had to pass through our bedroom to get to the front or rear of the apartment. The room was too small for a regular-sized bed and passageway so we always slept on a studio couch. I do not remember sleeping alone or in a conventional bed until Allan went into the Army.

The bathroom scene in the morning was a real comedy routine. We worked in pairs since we only had one bathroom. Pop was out of the house by the time the kids got up. I do not recall Mom ever using the bathroom in the morning. My sisters would go in first because they needed more time. How the girls managed I never figured out. When it was Allan's and my turn, one would wash while the other sat on the pot. If there was ever an emergency and I could not get into the bathroom, I would run two short blocks to the Shul on New Lots and Pennsylvania and use the facilities there.

Speaking of bathrooms reminds me of the annual experience before Passover. There was no bathing or showering for five days before Passover so that Mom could soak the glassware for three days to make them kosher for Pesach. Then for two days the whitefish and pike were swimming in the tub so we could have fresh gefilte fish.

I was enrolled in the public and Hebrew schools in the same year. I attended P.S. 190 from 9 until 3 and then Hebrew school at the New Lots Talmud Torah. I can still recall my grandfather, a very dignified gentleman with a long white beard, clasping my little hand and walking me to register for Hebrew school. This was my Zeyde's ritual. He proudly registered all his grandchildren that lived in the neighborhood for the first day of Hebrew school.

I attended Hebrew school five days a week, Monday through Thursday and Sunday. On weekdays, I went from 4 to 6 p.m. in the lower grades and 6 to 8 p.m. in the upper grades. Sunday classes were from 9 to 11 a.m.

I attended religious services on Friday nights, Saturday mornings, and Jewish holidays. I was a member of the Young Israel and a *shomer shabbas,* which meant I observed the Sabbath and dietary laws. This was a natural way of life in my house, especially with my father and brother Allan setting the example. My first contact with non-kosher food was when I was sixteen- or seventeen-years old. My sisters Esther and Belle took me to the local Chinese restaurant. I worried that G-d would strike me dead before I finished the meal.

⁓

When I was thirteen, Mom took me shopping for my Bar Mitzvah suit at Levinson's on Stone and Belmont Avenues. This was my first suit that came with long pants. Before that I only wore knickers. My Bar Mitzvah was at the New Lots Talmud Torah. We had my party in our apartment. The furniture was moved to the hallway and into the bedrooms. Pop set up wooden tables on carpenter horses in the dining and living rooms. As usual, Mom was the caterer. She did all the cooking and baking for the shindig.

Since I was born on Yom Kippur, my Zeyde bought me the honor of *Gelila,* tying the Torah before returning it to the ark. Such honors were auctioned off in those days. No one would dare bid against Zeyde because of the great respect they all showed for him. I had the honor of *Gelila* every Yom Kippur from the ages of thirteen to twenty-one, the year I went into the army.

⁓

We lived across the street from Carol's Ice Cream Parlor, the occasional hangout for some local hoods. I can recall Pal Silvers, a prizefighter and his boys, and Maxie Shapiro and his brothers. Most of them were eventually killed off in various gang wars. It was a common practice for these hoods to pitch nickels at the little kids on the block. One evening, I must have picked up at least five nickels. When Mom found out, she gave me holy hell for taking money from these gangsters. She wanted me to return the money. That was one of the few times I did not listen to my mother.

⁓

My household chores were minimal. Allan and I would usually take out the heavy cans of coal ashes from the furnace and carry up the ice for our icebox. We purchased the ice at the local dock and wheeled the ice home in a small handcart that Pop built.

The folks were firm believers in education. School and homework were the top priorities. Pop insisted that his boys go to college instead of following in his and his father's trade and end up as carpenters. As a deterrent, he would not allow us to assist him in any of his carpentry work.

Carpentry work was scarce in the Depression of the 1930s. Pop would report to various construction sites early in the morning and try to secure work. The individual union cards were drawn by lottery, and if Pop's card were selected, he would have the job.

Pop usually carried his toolbox with him, but on occasion he would not and then would call home if he got work. Since I was the last to leave for school, I was selected to deliver the toolbox. The box itself was made of solid wood. The weight with all the tools inside must have been at least a hundred pounds. At least as a kid it felt that heavy. The subway was five city blocks away. I had to stop every few hundred yards to rest and regroup. The thought of taking a bus or trolley never entered my mind. Walking was the standard mode of transportation except for long trips.

We all took turns taking Pop's handsaws to be sharpened. Since I was the youngest, I inherited the job permanently. I had no one to pass the job to. I would drop the saws off on Sunday morning and pick them up Sunday evening. I did not mind the job, except during winter, because crossing Linden Boulevard was an ordeal when it was cold and the wind was blowing.

The chore I liked the best was buying "charlotte russes" for the family. A "charlotte russe" was a delicate piece of pastry, consisting of sponge cake and whipped cream, with a cherry on top. It was packed in a round cardboard base with thin cardboard wrapping around the whole cake. It does not sound like much to brag about today, but it was delicious. I would walk five long, cross-town blocks to Sutter Avenue in the cold of winter to pick up six of these delicacies. The going price was five cents a piece at the local candy store. Mom sent me to the Sutter Avenue store, which was only open in the winter months, because the cakes were discounted at three cents.

We were creatures of habit when it came to food. We ate chicken Friday evenings. After Shul on Saturday, we ate chicken or *cholent*. In the evening, we brought in deli from Gorelick's. Sunday mornings we ate bagels, lox, and other smoked fish from Meyer's Appetizing across the street. Sunday dinner was usually *keinkletin,* a thick hamburger consisting of chopped meat, matzo meal, eggs, onions, salt, and pepper. Mom thought that chopped meat would fall apart during cooking without matzo meal and eggs. The *keinkletin* were fried in chicken fat with sautéed onions.

Mom would give me a nickel for my mid-morning snack at P.S. 190. Milk cost three cents a container. A graham cracker or Hydrox cookie was one cent each. My classmate Sammy Wohl would buy five cookies every day with his milk. In my eyes that was wealth.

I recall that my sixth grade teacher at P.S. 190 was Mr. Aronson, and one of the other sixth grade teachers was Mr. Gross. They loved to play handball, and they usually selected Fred Silverman and me, the best athletes in our grade, as their opponents. We beat them quite often.

Every spring we had a field day where students from all the public schools in the district participated in the sports events. When I was in 6B, I won the 60-yard dash, the only gold medal winner from my school. The school held a special auditorium assembly to present the awards. I felt like a real celebrity.

After completing the sixth grade at P.S. 190, I went to Junior High School 149 where I was accepted in the rapid advance program. We covered three years of school in two, including our freshman year of high school.

I then went to the Thomas Jefferson High School annex on Williams Avenue for one and a half years and spent my last one and a half years at the main building on Pennsylvania Avenue. Because I spent my high school career at three different locations and only my last three terms at the main building, my social life was limited.

～

Passover week was a difficult time for our digestion. All the matzoh, eggs, and meals fried in chicken fat were tough on the stomach. I think I am paying for it now with my stomach problems and high cholesterol. Can you imagine having a breakfast consisting of *fleisheke feinkachen,* an omelet fried in chicken fat, or sliced matzoh balls fried in shmaltz? No wonder Pop was always drinking his antacid concoction of bicarbonate of soda and vinegar.

～

Even with our tight schedule of public school and Hebrew classes, we still had plenty of time for games and playing ball. When we were kids we played "hyngo seek." I did not realize until I was a teenager that the actual name was "hide and go seek." We also played "kick the can and run the bases," "Johnny on the pony," and "ringo levio." To this day I do not know what "ringo levio" means.

We played our sports according to the season. Roller skating, hockey on roller skates, and football were played in the fall and winter. Since our playground was the street, we played touch football and association. Association was football with three men on a team. Each team had four downs to score a touchdown by running plays or throwing passes. The playing field was between the sewers on the street or the telephone poles on the sidewalks. Once a team scored a touchdown, three new players replaced the losing team.

Spring and summer were the big seasons when we played punchball, stickball, and softball. Every neighborhood had its own punchball team. We were the Pirates. Punchball was played with five men on each side. First and third base were on the street sides of the sidewalks. Second base was a sewer cover in the middle of the street. Positions were first base, third base, a center in front of second base, and two outfielders. The game was played with a pink Spalding high bouncer ball and without gloves. Our first team was Sidney (Snooky) Kamhi at first, Benny Golub at third, Bernard (Buggy) Goodman and Irving (Itzki) Habib in the outfield, and me, the center and team captain. We had short-sleeved gray jerseys with black borders. The name "Pirates" was sewn on the front, and our numbers were on the back. Our goal was to have club jackets, but we were never able to swing it.

Our main competitors were the boys from Georgia Avenue and the Royals, who were mainly Sephardic Jews. We called them Turks, because most of their parents came from Turkey. We usually played on par with the Georgia Avenue team, but the Royals were our patsies. Morris Acunis, one of my golf cronies when I lived in Palm Greens who played for the Royals, is under the mistaken impression that his team won a majority of the games. Jack Albala, another Floridian and former Royal, agrees with my version that the Pirates did most of the winning.

The stakes were a nickel a man, and both teams chipped in for the cost of the ten-cent ball. The game consisted of seven innings, and we usually played a double header. If we lost both games, which was not often, it meant we were out fifty cents and the cost of the ball. Financially, this was devastating.

Stickball was played with the same layout on the street as punchball, but instead of punching or slapping the ball, we used a broomstick handle for a bat. The ball was either a Spalding high bouncer or a tennis ball. Many a time we convinced our mothers that their brooms were worn out and that they needed to purchase new ones. A good stickball player was someone who could hit the ball two sewers. Depending on how the game was played, either the batter hit the ball himself or a pitcher threw it underhand on one bounce. The hitter then hit the ball with the stick. Most of the time we played among ourselves. The best players chose up sides. Unfortunately, the inferior players were picked last or not at all. That was the way it was done and nobody complained. Believe it or not, none of these kids grew up with psychological problems.

Softball was played in the local schoolyard. Gloves were in limited supply, so they were usually reserved for the catcher and first baseman. The game was played on cement fields, because grass and dirt fields were not available. The big trick was to be able to drop slide without tearing your pants and rear end.

Irving, the richest kid on the block, owned a football and a basketball. We played those sports when Irving wanted to play. If Irving was sick or not available, we reverted to other games where specialized equipment was not needed.

Ten to thirteen were my favorite years. The various public schools had organized sports programs. The emphasis was on competitive baseball and basketball games for kids under five-feet tall. Each playground had its own team, and they played the other school teams in tournament play. Fortunately, I was good enough to make the teams. This was my first opportunity to play with quality equipment and on reserved playing fields or courts. The most difficult part was measuring in under five-feet tall. Some of the players really slouched and surreptitiously bent over during the measurements. Once the games started, they suddenly were way above the height limitation.

When we were teenagers, P.S. 182 was the home of the local evening social and sports center. It offered basketball, volleyball, and ping-pong. We entered our team in the various basketball tournaments. There was no adult supervision. The elected captains picked the teams and made the substitutions. The object was to win so the best kids played. Sidney "Sonny" Bernstein would sneak away from the boys and play ping-pong. He was the corner champion.

Very few of the boys could afford bicycles. I never owned a bike, not even a tricycle. But we all knew how to ride. We usually rented bicycles from the Bike Store on Riverdale and Alabama Avenues for fifteen cents an hour. We would pedal to Highland Park and back for a few hours of fun and exercise.

Traveling to Coney Island by subway required taking the IRT subway to Franklin Avenue and then changing to the BMT for a slow, hot, and long subway ride. My friend Irving received a car as a high school graduation present, and occasionally Buggy was able to borrow his father's car. On those days we traveled in style. But most often we hitchhiked to the beach. Hitchhiking was acceptable and safe in our day. We would stand on the corner of Pennsylvania and Linden Boulevard and accept a ride in any direction towards the beach. If we were lucky, we would get a direct ride on the Belt Parkway. The longer alternative routes took us down Linden Boulevard or Flatbush Avenue to Ocean Parkway and the beach. A trip to Coney Island always included frankfurters at Nathan's. We always wore our bathing suits under our street clothes. To change after a day at the beach, we would make a circle under the boardwalk, remove our bathing suits, and put on our street clothes. An alternative method was to stop an elevator between floors in one of the apartment houses on Ocean Parkway to change clothes.

When we were young teenagers, our ambition was to be allowed into the pool hall. We were all baseball fanatics, and in those days, ticker tape was used to relay the play-by-play. The older boys would yell out the ticker scores, and we would keep track by inning using chalk on the sidewalk.

When we reached about sixteen years of age, we were finally allowed in and started playing pool. Moishe's Pool Room was above the Biltmore Theater on New Lots and Vermont Avenues. Bab's Pool Hall was on the corner of New Lots and Hinsdale. Both "gentlemen" were also the local bookies. There is a universal quote: "Show me a good pool player and I'll show you a misspent youth."

When we were growing up, "corner" was an important word in our vocabulary. We actually were referring to two corners, the southwest and northwest corners of Hegeman and Pennsylvania Avenues. On the southwest corner Barney's Candy store was on Pennsylvania Avenue and Nathan's Barber Shop was on Hegeman Avenue. On the northwest corner we had Doc Abrams Pharmacy on Hegeman Avenue and Eisenberg's Candy Store on the Pennsylvania Avenue side.

back row: Bernard Rosenthal, Bernard (Buggy) Goodman, Murray (Moishe)
Finkel, Lou (Chink) Heckelman
middle row: Bernard (Bookie) Feirstein, Dave (Davie) Plaxe
front row: Paul Wasserman, Ben (Bennie) Golub

Nathan Miller, our local barber, was the neighborhood character. I always thought that he was an awful barber but since he was inexpensive, he did a good business. He washed his own towels and had a different price for each customer. Every haircut included a dirty story.

Doc Abrams was a very concerned and respected individual. He was our father confessor and dispenser of free condoms. When we were too young to use them, we carried them in our wallets. We all had the same raised circular outline of the rubber in our wallets. After some of the boys got married years later, some of their wives gave birth nine months into their marriages. This raised the possibility that Doc was handing out seconds. I refer especially to Sonny and Dinah.

The corner was the hangout, message center, and assembly point for five different age groups of approximately ten to fifteen members. The age differential was about two years between groups, and the age span was the early teens to late twenties. We also had a few boys who fell between the cracks or were just not joiners.

Few of us had home phones when we were growing up. One's social life, especially for the girls, depended on getting a phone call at Doc's Pharmacy or one of the two candy stores. A good tip for being called to the phone was a nickel. Phil Leff's sister Chavie was a great tipper. The poor tippers often would not be paged or get their messages.

Since Barney's was a larger store, we usually hung out at his place. After Barney sold out, we switched our allegiance to Eisenberg's across the street. We usually assembled outside the stores, since if too many of us were inside at one time, there was no room for the cash customers. We had an agreement with management. We could enter the store to make a purchase, use the phone, or take or leave a message. This agreement usually worked well, but there were problems in inclement weather.

There were at least three nut machines outside every candy store: sunflower seeds, pumpkin seeds, and India nuts. A penny in the slot would get you a handful of nuts. Since we started to assemble each evening around seven, by nine o'clock there would be an inch of shells in front of the store. The income from the machines helped pay the store's rent. Steve Hornick was the champ for both total consumption and speed.

As young teenagers, sports were the main topic of conversation. We would argue the merits of the Brooklyn Dodgers, New York Giants, and New York Yankees for hours on end. As we grew older and started to date, the conversation naturally switched to girls. On Sunday mornings we bragged about our conquests, spoke about our almost victories or just-missing-by-a-hair's, and laughed about our complete failures. Listening to the older fellows describe their Saturday night dates and evenings at the Gayheart, Mayfair, and Dome dance halls was a great growing up experience. It is too bad I do not have the conversations on tape.

On Sunday mornings, all the groups assembled in the schoolyard for our weekly softball games. You played until your team lost. Sometimes we played a triple header.

The Cellar Club was an extension of the corner. The club was located at the corner of Vermont and Riverdale in the basement of a four-family house. The finished part of the cellar was the clubroom, with a room in the back for our card games and an open clothes closet for coats. The rear of the cellar contained the furnace, which was off limits. The monthly rent was about twelve dollars. We usually had a tough time coming up with the payment.

back row: Bloom (Bloomie), Murray (Moishe) Finkel, Herman (Cousin or Chaim) Rubin
front row: Dave (Davie) Plaxe, Ben (Bennie) Golub

The club originated with the older boys. As each age group started to marry or go into the military, the next age group would take over the operation. There was no purchase agreement. The only stipulation was that the remaining members of the prior group would maintain visiting privileges. During the war years, the club members consisted of boys too young to serve and the fellows from all the groups who were medically deferred. All the boys who were home on furlough were honorary members.

Each group had its own club name. We called ourselves Club Raleigh. I believe the runner-up choice was "Do Drop In." The decorations were simple. There were couches against the walls, a radio, a record player, and blue and red lighting behind the furniture. The walls were painted whatever color was available. The shade did not make much of a difference since the room was always dark.

The couches were old and very fragile. The only time you were allowed to put your feet on the furniture was when you were socializing with a girl. If the necking became hot and heavy, and you could convince the boys that you might make out, it was their obligation to leave the club or go into the card room and close the door.

The colored bulbs were always blowing out. Thanks to the Biltmore Theater, we had a very accessible supply. Buggy was responsible for keeping our place properly lit.

We were always in financial trouble. The twelve dollars monthly rent was an exorbitant amount for boys going to school or just starting their working careers. To help pay the rent, we would have Open House Friday Night with a twenty-five cents admission. Of course it was free for the girls. If we were still short, we emptied our pockets or borrowed a few dollars from the older fellows on the corner. Our biggest fundraiser was our annual raffle. We charged ten cents and would advertise a price valued at about fifty dollars. Fortunately, the printer would always omit the date and location of the drawing.

When the war broke out, most of the boys from the corner were either drafted or volunteered. For a while we were running farewell parties every weekend at the club. When Club Raleigh could no longer operate because most of our members were in the service, we turned the place over to Phil Leff and his group. After the war, we went back to the corner, but something was missing. We were no longer kids, but mature men who grew up in a hurry the hard way. The corner was the hangout for a while, but now there was little differentiation between age groups. In a few years most of the boys became engaged, married, and moved away.

I kept close relationships with Dave Plaxe, Sonny Bernstein, and Buggy Goodman. I restored my acquaintance with Paul Wasserman when my son Andy moved to Maryland. These are my oldest and best friends, and I will always love them.

In August 1988, Buggy, Dave, Phil, and I arranged a reunion of the boys from the corner. The party was on Long Island, and about forty of the original boys came. About seventy people came in total from as far away as Florida, Arizona, California, and Hong Kong. Some of us had not seen each other in forty-five years. We cried, hugged, and kissed. A great time was had by all.

Red, Marty (Mooky) Flam, Abe (Jap) Rosenblum, Irving (Itzkl) Habib, Red Posner, Bernard (Buggy) Goodman, Sid (Sonny) Bernstein, Irving (Ike) Broderson, Bernard Rosenthall, Ben (Benny) Golub, Dave (Davie) Plaxe, Murray (Moishe) Finkel

Muriel Leff, Murray Finkel, Phil Leff

Left to right: Dave Plaxe, unknown, Roz Plaxe, Dotty Finkel, Murray Finkel, Abe Rosenblum, Shirley Rosenblum

I would like to dedicate *Growing Up in Brooklyn* to Dave Plaxe and Bernard (Buggy) Goodman. Unfortunately, Dave passed away in January 1990 and Buggy in March 1992. We were friends from the age of seven and grew up together. We played ball, socialized, hung around the corner, and belonged to the same club. When I was in the Army, Dave was in the Navy, and Buggy was in the Coast Guard. We continuously corresponded with each other. Buggy even visited me in the Army hospital in Rome, Georgia, after I was wounded.

After the war, we did the singles scene together, double and triple dated. We all became engaged and married within a short time of each other. We were ushers at each other's weddings. We celebrated our children's B'nai Mitzvahs and weddings together. We attended each other's parents' funerals and made our respective Shiva visits.

When I became sick in 1989 and was on chemotherapy, the boys continuously called from New York. Dave called me in Florida every week, and when I remarked that I would call him the next week, he said, "Don't you dare, I will call you."

Dave and Bernie were two of my oldest friends. I will miss them always.

Dave Plaxe, Murray Finkel, Bernard Goodman

BERNARD GOODMAN: MY PAL BUGGY

By Murray I. Finkel

Bernard Goodman, better known as Buggy, was one of my oldest and dearest friends. This piece is not meant to be derogatory. I would never say or write anything to hurt or besmirch the memory of Buggy. I loved him like a brother, and everything I write is just my attempt to describe his behavior and his eccentricities.

Buggy was known for his strange shtick. One day he did something peculiar that I don't now even recall offhand. I remarked, "You nutty bug." That's how the nickname Buggy originated. Why did he do these way out things? Who knows? Probably he wanted to be noticed. Once he started, he loved the attention and therefore had to continue to maintain his reputation.

We all had nicknames. The most interesting names were Buggy, Chink, Jap, Mookey, The Mayor, Babe, Tex, and Sonny. The name I loved most was Killer. Buggy's brother Sidney had a hernia. The Yiddish word for hernia is *killah*. There were also nicknames that had Jewish derivations. Those were Moishe, Feivie, Itzki, Shmoolik and others. The nickname that stuck to the end was Buggy. As adults when I started to call him Bernard, he used to say, "To you, I'll always be Buggy." In this piece though, I'll use the names Buggy and Bernard interchangeably.

Actually, Buggy and I were complete opposites. The things we had in common were our love of sports, our respect for each other, and the fact that we enjoyed spending time together. We were just pals. I presume there must have been other intangibles since our friendship lasted more than sixty years.

Buggy was the best athlete on the corner. If World War II hadn't disrupted our lives and he was a little more serious and dedicated,

Bernard could have been a professional baseball player. Unfortunately, Thomas Jefferson High School didn't have a baseball team, and there was no one available to help him develop his talents.

Bernard was the best at sports in our group. I was second best in our group but not even close to Buggy in ability. We therefore usually chose up sides, so we rarely played on the same team. When we played as the "Pirates" as the corner team, or played against the older boys, it was a pleasure and honor to be on his side. He was really outstanding.

Buggy and I played on the same team on the public school summer softball league. You had to measure in under five feet to qualify. Bernard was about five feet two inches, but he had a knack of slouching and bending surreptitiously while being measured.

During our high school days, the big football game was Jefferson vs. Tilden, and it was played on Thanksgiving Day. We usually rented a horse and wagon, and we all piled in. Buggy was the official driver, since he was the biggest and strongest and could handle the horse.

One Thanksgiving Day, we were waiting for Bernard to show up. It was not like him to be late. He finally arrived with a big smile and his two front teeth broken. He was playing touch football on Georgia Avenue, and someone elbowed him in the mouth. A normal mortal would go home, ice his mouth, and bemoan his bad luck. Not Buggy. He was needed to drive the horse and wagon, and he had to be there.

The horse and wagon were always available if we needed some furniture for our Cellar Club. We would go anywhere if we heard some relative or friend was disposing of furniture. Buggy was always available to drive. During our meetings at Club Raleigh, we were always short of money and had difficulty in meeting our monthly rent. To protect the fragile furniture, shoes were not permitted on the couches. Feet on the furniture or cursing during a meeting were both subject to fines. Bernard would purposefully ignore the warnings and get fined. When I asked him why he was so obstinate, he would say that the Club needed the money and this was his contribution.

When we were playing poker in someone's home and later in the Club, Buggy would work his favorite shtick. When he was shy during the betting, he would take the shy money out of the pot and set the money aside. If he lost, instead of making change to pay off his losses, he would conveniently not return the shy money to the pot. At the end of the evening, he usually reimbursed the winner of the pot that was shortchanged.

Bernard was the first to get a driver's license. His father had a car that he used in business, and since Buggy helped out on occasion, he had access to the family auto. I recall that I went along with Bernard on a trip to East Flatbush in order to pick up a check from one of his father's customers. I waited in the car about forty-five minutes. When I asked why it took him so long, he replied that the customer wasn't home, so he made out with the maid. Buggy was a little crude in his approach to women. He didn't believe in wasting time, and he usually came right to the point. Bernard was slapped in the face very often, but he made out the most.

He was the first to volunteer for military service. The boys used to visit him at the Coast Guard Boot Camp at Manhattan Beach.

On one occasion during the war, Buggy and Phil were visiting in the Catskills, and they ran short of ration cards to purchase gasoline. Buggy siphoned enough gasoline from my Uncle Bernie's Cadillac to make it back to Brooklyn.

After the war, Buggy went to some watch repair school under the G.I. Bill. I gave him a watch to repair that I confiscated from a German prisoner. That was the last I saw of the watch. I believe Bernard dropped the works on the floor.

Before I was married, Buggy, his date, Dotty, and I had tickets to the Rangers hockey game. We were late, so we grabbed a fast bite at the Garden Cafeteria. Bernard ordered something with rice, and it looked awful. When I inquired why he wasn't eating his rice, he answered, "I don't drink plain milk either." I interpreted the profound statement as meaning that he didn't like plain rice but enjoyed eating friend rice in a Chinese restaurant. He also did not like drinking plain milk but loved milk with chocolate syrup. The girls were astonished and acted as if I were Joseph interpreting Pharaoh's dreams. I don't think anyone understood Buggy as well as I did.

Buggy, Dotty, and I went shopping for Father's Day gifts on Pitkin Avenue. We probably went to Ripley's or Crawford's. The stores were always on opposite corners. After looking around for a while, we were still undecided about what to buy. Buggy removed a jacket from the rack, put it on, and said, "Why don't you buy your father a jacket like this one?" He then walked out of the store. I thought Dotty was going to pass out.

We visited Abe and Shirley Rosenblum in their first apartment on St. Mark's Place in Brooklyn. It was a two-bedroom apartment and the second bedroom was empty. Buggy came late to the party with his date. He had picked up this long-distance operator while making a phone call. He made out on four bridge chairs in the spare room. Only Buggy could pick up an operator and make out under those conditions.

During the years that he was driving his cab, there wasn't a taxi driver that didn't know Buggy. He bought a car wash with Bert, and many a customer would tell the cashier that he was a friend of Buggy's and not pay for the car wash.

In August 1988, with the help of Buggy, Dave, and Phil, we arranged a reunion in Long Island with the boys from the corner of Pennsylvania and Hegeman Avenues. Buggy was a tiresome worker. He would thumb through the phone books looking for familiar names so he could inform them about the reunion.

In Florida, if I ran across someone from the old neighborhood, he always inquired about Buggy. Everyone remembered and loved Buggy.

Unfortunately, Buggy passed away in March 1992. When he wasn't feeling well, I used to beg him to take his medicine. He used to say that he felt fine, but promised to take the medication. Obviously he didn't. Bernard did not believe in doctors.

We started our friendship when we were seven-years old and grew up together as kids. We played ball, socialized, hung around the corner, and belonged to the same club. During my stay in the Army and Buggy's in the Coast Guard, we continuously corresponded with one another. After the war, we did the singles scene together and double dated. We became engaged and married within a short time of each other. We were ushers together and celebrated our children's Bar and Bat Mitzvahs. We attended each other's parents' funerals and made our respective Shiva visits. When I became sick in 1989 and was taking chemotherapy, Buggy was continuously in touch with me from New York.

Buggy was one of my oldest and best friends, and he would give you the shirt off his back. He was a *Gutte Neshameh*, a good soul. I loved him, and I will always miss him.

MY WAR MEMORIES

By Murray I. Finkel

Rome, '44
Italy

On October 2, 1942, on my twentieth birthday, I was subject to the draft. I was in my senior year at the College of the City of New York, School of Business and Civic Administration, now known as the Bernard M. Baruch College. I joined the Enlisted Reserve Corps (ERC) for students attending college, hoping not to be called until I finished school. Unfortunately, the ERC at my college was called up in February 1943 and we were to report to active duty in the army in April 1943.

The college set a policy that allowed a student with enough credits in his major to normally graduate in June to double or triple up in his major in classroom hours until he was called up in April. All minor subject courses could be dropped from the schedule. I was fortunate enough to have enough accounting credits to qualify for my B.B.A. degree which I received in June 1943 while I was already in the army.

I reported to Camp Upton, in Suffolk County, New York, in April 1943. Today the site is the home of the Brookhaven National Laboratory. I was then assigned to Camp Wolters, Mineral Wells, Texas, an infantry replacement training center.

Five of us from City College were assigned to the same battalion in Camp Wolters. Four of us had enough credits to get our degree, but the fifth was short credits so he did not graduate. Naturally, he was a bit depressed. A few weeks into basic training there was a call for applicants for the Army Student Training Program (ASTP). The commanding officer was under the mistaken impression that the program was only for undergraduates. Our buddy who did not finish his degree qualified. His depression quickly disappeared with the news that this additional training would put him back in the classroom and out of the infantry.

Basic training was tough, but since I was in good shape physically I had no difficulty in completing my thirteen weeks. Being Jewish I had to prove to myself that I was as good or better than the other soldiers.

Most of the troops were from diversified backgrounds with limited education. I remember Hawkins, from the hills of Arkansas, once made a derogatory remark about Jews. Jack Goldberg, a street-smart bookie from Brooklyn, practically lifted him off the ground with a blow to the jaw. Hawkins, lying on the floor, asked, "Why did Goldberg hit me?" Told that Goldberg was Jewish, he was surprised and admitted that he did not know any Jews back home. He thought that Jew bastard was one word.

We had a coal miner from West Virginia who never showered. Can you imagine the odor in the barracks after weeks in the hot Texas sun participating in intensive basic training? He was warned to bathe or receive a GI shower. He disregarded the warning and four soldiers with stiff brushes and GI bars of brown soap scrubbed him down. He was a bloody mess. A few weeks later he received another GI shower. Even though the coal miner was illiterate, he was not dumb. He eventually received his discharge from the army.

There was also a prizefighter from Pittsburgh with a body like Adonis who was assigned permanent latrine orderly. He was purposely wetting his bed and was also discharged from the service. One of the recruits would also fake collapsing after a few hundred yards of hiking. He also received his walking papers. I never tried to beat the army by attempting to get out. Maybe I was just too young and innocent.

While on the machine gun range I was continuously hitting the target. I really did not want to qualify as an expert machine gunner. The weapon was too heavy and dangerous to lug around. I also recalled the scene from the movie "Sergeant York," when the German officer yelled, "Eliminate that machine gun nest!" It just so happened that I missed the target on my next few rounds. I did qualify, though, as an expert rifleman.

On one of our bivouac exercises, we had to simulate battle conditions. I had to dig my foxhole before I could bed down for the night. I thought I was lucky to find an easy digging location. I completed the hole and placed my equipment in it and lay down for some much-needed rest. I then felt something sticking me in the back. It was an old sign covered up with dirt that said "Latrine" and the date. I had to dig a new trench.

I received a few weekend passes into Mineral Wells, the closest town to camp. We called it Venereal Wells because of the large number of social diseases the boys picked up.

I graduated after thirteen weeks of intensive training. Unfortunately, an accounting degree did not elicit a transfer to another outfit for additional specialization or schooling. Since I was a replacement I was stuck in the infantry. I eventually was assigned to a division on my first day of combat. It was practically impossible to transfer out of a fighting unit.

After basic training I went home for a week furlough and then reported back to Camp Wolters for three days. I was then sent to Camp Shenango, Pennsylvania, an assembly area for about ten days. There I learned how to plant sod on the street in front of the barracks. I did get an overnight pass and decided to visit my aunt and cousins in Cleveland. The bus broke down on the way and we were delayed about two hours until a replacement arrived. All my cousins who were assembled at my aunt's house for my arrival said that they passed the bus on the side of the road but never thought to check out the soldiers who were standing beside it.

My next stop was Hampton Roads, Virginia, a point of embarkation for overseas duty. After about a week we boarded the troop ship, the Louis Pasteur, a converted luxury liner. The ship was sunk a few trips later. Being replacements, the lowest of the low, we had the worst accommodations. I presume it was similar to steerage. We were assigned hammocks, but most of us slept on the floor. We were allowed to go topside a few hours a day to exercise, or were assigned to some work detail. Most of the trip we were seasick.

We finally landed in September 1943 in Casablanca, Morocco. I received an eight-hour pass to attend Rosh Hashanah services. That was the extent of my sightseeing in Casablanca. I recall the Arab men wearing cutout barracks bags, the army version of duffel bags, as trousers. Holes were made in the legs and the drawstring held up the pants. The women walked in front of the men. That way, if there were a mine, the female would be the one to be blown up.

In Casablanca we boarded a French troop train called a "forty and eight," so named because it carried *quarante hommes ou huit chevaux,* 40 men or 8 horses. Our diet consisted of cold "C" rations. The menu was meat and beans, meat and vegetable hash, or meat and vegetable stew. Most of the soldiers preferred the meat and beans. While traveling through the African desert with a primary diet of meat and beans, we had a choice of suffocating with the doors closed or freezing at night with the doors open. About a week later, we finally arrived in Bizerte, on the African coast in northern Tunisia, tired and dirty.

In Bizerte we loaded onto a landing craft infantry (LCI) naval ship for the last stage of our trip to Naples, Italy. I spent about a week at an infantry replacement depot waiting to be assigned to a division. At this camp ranger and paratrooper representatives tried to convince the young replacements to volunteer for their respective combat outfits. The officers were All-American types—tall and blonde with GI haircuts and combat boots. The boots were very impressive because the infantrymen wore leggings. We were harangued, cursed, yelled at, called yellow bellies, and dared to volunteer for the rangers or paratroopers. They did some "con job" on these replacements. The infantry was dangerous enough for me.

In October 1943 I was assigned to the Third Battalion, Fifteenth Regiment of the Third Division. The Regiment was General George Marshal's and Dwight Eisenhower's old unit. We were always reminded of the honor to serve in such a distinguished outfit. It was also the Regiment of Audie Murphy, war hero, Congressional Medal of Honor recipient, and later movie star. The Third Division had distinguished itself in World War I. Before I joined the Division, its men had already made the invasions of North Africa, Sicily, and parts of Italy.

The non-commissioned officers (non coms) were mostly career army men and great soldiers but usually ignorant and bigoted. The draftees and replacements were of a different breed. Many of the career soldiers were alcoholics, would drink anything, and have sex with any female.

We had some real characters in my company. I recall one of the mess sergeants making his own concoction of moonshine. He would mix rubbing alcohol, lemon extract, and after-shave lotion. Then he would strain this so-called drink through some brown shoe polish to give it the color of whiskey or scotch.

One of the Staff Sergeants, a great soldier, had contracted a venereal disease at least five times. He was broken in rank each time but always restored to Sergeant because he was the best non com in the company. When asked why he did not use a condom, he responded, "Would you wash your feet with your socks on?"

Tater Hill, an old souse from South Carolina, had no teeth, spoke with a deep southern accent, and had a terrific sense of humor. He used to say that the next best thing to a woman is a sheep. He'd say that you lead the sheep to the edge of a cliff and place her hind legs in your high boots. As you're pushing forward, the sheep is pushing back. But you must be careful and fast because after the sheep comes, she usually shits. To this day I do not know if he was serious or pulling my leg.

Most of the non coms served in the army during the Depression. They usually came from small towns, the hill country, or farms. I had three prerequisites for being on their shit list. I was Jewish, a college graduate, and my hometown was New York City. I pulled the most kitchen police (KP) and guard duty in my platoon.

I recall when I was assigned to my Division as a replacement, my First Sergeant asked how many of us were Jewish. I was the only one who raised my hand. Pop Bailey, my Platoon Sergeant, came from the hills of Arkansas. He once showed me a spread in LIFE magazine depicting foundling babies left on the doorsteps of St. Patrick's Cathedral in

New York City. "What kind of city do you come from?" he asked. I responded, "Most of the mothers of those kids came from the Ozarks, were knocked up at thirteen, and came to New York to get lost." Not very diplomatic on my part.

Most of the anti-Semitism originated from the non coms, but sometimes the enlisted men were just as guilty. Sometimes when we marched my fellow soldiers sang, "Onward Christian soldiers, let the Jews buy the war bonds." It really burned me up. Another time, when we were caught in an artillery barrage, one of my so-called buddies remarked, within my hearing distance, "If it was not for the Jews and that Roosevelt Jew, we would not be in this predicament." I lost my temper and swung my rifle as a baseball bat at his head. If someone had not pushed me during my swing, I would have bashed in his skull.

There was a dramatic change in my personal army life after we were off the front lines for a few days of rest and relaxation. I responded to a call for tryouts for the Battalion baseball team and I was fortunate enough to make the team as a shortstop. From that day on, my lifestyle changed. The first baseman was the Supply Sergeant and the catcher was the Mess Sergeant. I finally earned some respect. There was a time when I used to beg for an extra pair of socks. Now I was not only offered socks, but also shoes and other garments by my new buddy the Supply Sergeant. When I pulled KP, I was no longer cleaning pots and pans but dishing out the food. Unfortunately, we never actually played any baseball games because we were never off the lines long enough to schedule any games. When we pulled back, we usually took intensive training for the next invasion or campaign.

It seems that sports were the only equalizer where race or religion was concerned. One's playing ability was the main factor. After I was married and had children, I tried to impress on my two boys the value of sports in the real world. Fortunately they were good athletes and loved playing ball. Also, life in the infantry would have been different if I knew how to type. There were always calls for typists, but I could not qualify. I also insisted that Andy and Gary learn to type.

When I was assigned to the Third Division I joined the outfit in the mountain passes around Cassino, Italy. The Germans had gun emplacements in the abbey at Mount Cassino. They were shelling us and we could not fire back or bomb because of the holiness of the structure. After incurring excessive casualties we finally received permission to shell and bomb. We finally captured the abbey, and rumors to the contrary, there were actual gun positions located there.

It rained continuously during my stay at the Cassino front. We were knee high in mud and always wet and cold. So much for sunny Italy. I did learn how to maneuver down the muddy paths in the mountains. The trick was to walk pigeon-toed to avoid falling and sliding down on your fanny.

In December 1943 we were pulled off the Cassino lines. We were trucked back to a wooded area outside Pozzuoli, on the Italian Riviera, about twenty miles north of Naples. We pitched our tents and then had three weeks of intensive amphibious training for the impending invasion of Anzio. We had vigorous infantry training in the morning, including a ten-mile speed march before lunch. On the ten-minute break some of the boys would have sex with the prostitutes. They knew our exact marching route and were always waiting for the soldiers.

In the afternoon we were trucked down to Naples. We practiced climbing down the rope ladders from the side of the ship into Higgins boats, the assault crafts that open in the front and hit the beaches. I recall Powell, a buddy of mine, descending the rope ladder and then puking every time he would hit the bottom of the moving Higgins boat. We repeated this descent about twenty or thirty times each afternoon. Each time Powell hit the moving boat he would vomit. He had a reserved spot on the boat. After a while he would turn green.

We performed these exercises with the British Navy. After one of our practice runs our Higgins boat started to sink. We were eventually picked up by an American Navy ship and ferried back to Naples. As the platoon assembled on the dock we broke out our rations. Our picture was taken by YANK Magazine, graced its cover, and was later copied by CORONET and other publications. The caption said it was taken after the Anzio invasion, but it was actually taken before a practice run. I am the third from the top left.

These, then, are the same doughboys . . . the fighting infantry from Iowa and California and Alabama and Manhattan . . . the men behind the blue stars . . . and the gold stars.

I did get one twelve-hour pass in Naples as a reward for being a good soldier.

We spent a week on an English ship waiting for the task force to assemble for the Anzio invasion. The British food was awful and the sleeping accommodations were worse. The incessant music from the bagpipes drove us crazy. We could not wait for the invasion to start.

I was given a bangalore torpedo, a charge of explosives attached to a long bamboo stick. It was my job to crawl on my stomach, light a charge and slip the torpedo into the slit of one of the pillboxes (square cement barricades with slits for firing machineguns) that we anticipated would be on the beachhead. Unfortunately, we hit some bad weather and the bangalore torpedo accidentally fell overboard.

The invasion started at 6 a.m. on January 22, 1944. The temperature was about 20 degrees. I was in the first wave and the British dropped us off about 100 yards from the beach up to our necks in water. We had little opposition, but we waded in frozen stiff. We were not allowed to stop and change into dry clothes because there was concern that the Germans would counter or bring in new troops from Rome. We walked around in circles until the sun came out and finally dried us out.

The mission of the Third Division, the First British Division, and a few ranger battalions was to debark on beaches north and south of Nettuno and Anzio. This area was in a line about twenty-five miles south of Rome. We were to trap the Germans between Rome and Cassino. Few foresaw the bitter five months with us stalemated on the beachhead. The Germans brought part of their forces from Rome to the mountains beyond the beach and we were trapped between the mountains and the sea.

Our casualties were unbelievable. Nothing happened in the daytime because the Germans had all our positions zeroed in. If anything moved, they shelled us unmercifully. All activity, including patrolling, laying mines, moving food and equipment, and evacuating the wounded was done at night. If you had to relieve yourself during the daytime you did it in your helmet, threw the mess along with your helmet outside your dugout or foxhole, and retrieved and cleaned your helmet that night.

The few prisoners we captured were of the elite African Corps. They were arrogant and obnoxious. They claimed that since the Germans were winning the war, we would soon be their prisoners.

The battle was going so poorly that I was given a charge of explosives and assigned the job of blowing up the last bridge on the beachhead before evacuating. When I inquired as to why I was the lucky one to be assigned this detail, I was told that I have the reputation of being a fast runner so I was the best qualified.

Many times during a barrage I would jump into the Mussolini Canal, which was basically an irrigation ditch, or various other ditches that covered the beachhead to avoid being hit by shrapnel. It was a miracle that I got off the Anzio beach without being wounded. It may have been that I was extremely lucky, or from the extra good luck from the money Mom put in the *pushke*.

I recall that I was one of two soldiers assigned to guard the medics because the Germans were infiltrating and capturing them. When we got to the medics quarters, which was a bombed-out barn, there was no place for us to bed down. When I was not assigned to walk guard duty I tried sleeping in the haystack. I found it too itchy and uncomfortable and I went back into the barn. About five minutes later a shell landed in the haystack, killing all the soldiers who were in that area. Again, the luck was with me.

A few of the boys in my squad and I were missing in action for about three days. We were on patrol and temporarily caught behind the German lines. We could not get back to our outfit. One dark and moonless night, we appropriated an abandoned American ambulance, took a circuitous route, and returned to our unit. Actually, the three days was not a bad deal. Being off the front lines, we were able to make a fire and heat our C rations. It was also the only time in Anzio that I did not have guard duty.

Land mines were everywhere in Anzio. If a cow were unfortunate enough to get blown up, we would retrieve the remains at night. One of the farm boys would skin the cow and we would dine on steak. Rabbit was also a hot item on our menu. It tasted like tough chicken. Anything was preferably to C rations.

Cleanliness was also a problem. The portable showers were rarely available. We would wash and shave out of our helmets. We called it a whore bath. Clean clothes were difficult to come by. Food medicine, mail, and evacuating the wounded had a higher priority. I remember wearing the same shirt for more than thirty consecutive days. I would rinse out the collar and put the shirt back on while the collar was still wet. I had two pairs of socks and nursed them along gingerly.

In one of my frequent letters to the folks, I made an offhand comment that I really could use a handkerchief. When our packages arrived, and they usually came in bunches, enclosed were about six dozen handkerchiefs. During the war, handkerchiefs were rationed and worth their weight in gold. Since I could not wash the hankies I discarded them like tissues. I can visualize what must have happened. My sister Esther probably gave the letter to my Uncle Abe to read, and he immediately brought them home from Premier Textile where he was one of the partners.

Speaking of packages, I can recall receiving one that included a package of sunflower seeds. When I started to eat them by cracking the seeds between my teeth, I attracted an audience. The boys thought I was doing magic. When they tried to emulate my performance, they began to choke and cough. No one can crack nuts like we Brooklyn kids with a corner background.

In anticipation of breaking through Anzio and continuing on to Rome, the combat troops took positions on the inside bank of the Mussolini Canal and the other ditches on the beachhead. We were dressed in full combat gear and complete field packs. The Air Force, artillery, and navy guns in the harbor shelled the German positions for about an hour. I slept through the entire barrage. I was always tired. We overran the German positions in the mountains overlooking our beachhead. Except for a few stragglers that we took as prisoners, the Germans left their fortified bunkers in a hurry. They left behind pistols, field glasses, blankets, sleeping bags, wine and food, cooking stoves, and other items of value. Unfortunately, we could not gamble and pick up these prizes of war because some of the bunkers were booby-trapped. Going into the bunkers was like playing Russian roulette. Some of the boys went in and were lucky, but others were blown up. I was not a gambling man.

My regiment was the first outfit to liberate Rome on June 5, 1944. Since the Pope declared Rome an open city, all combat troops were required to bivouac outside the city limits. It destroyed us to see the rear echelon of noncombatants come in behind us and garrison in Rome proper. Some of the soldiers received a week of "R and R"—rest and relaxation. Unfortunately, my turn never came. I did get a twelve-hour pass to visit Rome.

After about two weeks on the outskirts of Rome we were trucked back to the wooded area outside of Pozzouli. Again we participated in intensive amphibious training for our next invasion.

We were issued two-piece fatigue outfits to be worn during our training. While in combat or on the lines the dress was olive drab (OD).

Since the Germans wore green fatigues we only wore our OD's so we would not be mistaken for the enemy. There was almost a catastrophe on the lines when some of our replacements were shot as they were approaching our positions. Some of them goofed and mistakenly wore their fatigues.

I always wanted the one-piece overall fatigues. They looked macho. The only ones who were issued the one-piece fatigues were those in the motor pool. I managed to negotiate a trade with one of the drivers. But that night, on the way to the latrine, I realized that I had to slip out of the fatigues in order to go. As I was saddling the latrine slit trench, I looked down and I was making all over my sleeves. I gently slid out of my pant legs and walked bare ass back to my tent.

Wearing our fatigues and just taking it easy.

We were fortunate enough to make the invasion of southern France with the U.S. Navy where the food was delicious and we did not have to listen to bagpipes. In the early morning of August 15, 1944, I landed with the first wave of my platoon on the beaches of St. Tropez. This time our navy dropped us off on the beach. We barely got our feet wet. I must have been fortunate to have had the opportunity to spend the winter on the Italian Riviera and the summer on the French Riviera.

The invasion was a complete surprise to the Germans. We landed in the middle of a minefield, but the signs were still in place. We were all scared stiff to move out. Our captain ordered one of the lieutenants to lead us out of the minefield. He was nicknamed Lil' Abner because of his resemblance to the cartoon character. His size 14 shoes were convenient in leading us through this dangerous area. We all walked in his footsteps and fortunately the casualties were minimal.

We fought our way north until we hit the Vosges Mountains. Two of us were assigned to escort our Colonel back to our rear lines. He was being relieved because of some medical problems. He was a strapping six-footer and only carried side arms. My buddy and I were both shorter in height and were fully loaded down, with full field pack and rifles. He started to lead us, following the red telephone wire that was laid by the Germans, instead of the black wire laid by the Americans. I said, "Sir, we have been assigned to escort you back, so please follow us." We were only a few miles from Switzerland. I could have spent the balance of the war in the confines of a beautiful Swiss hotel, with the compliments of the U.S. government, if I had followed the Colonel and continued on to Switzerland.

On another occasion we captured some Germans. Because of my knowledge of Yiddish, which is somewhat similar to German, I did the interrogating. When I asked one of the prisoners for his watch, he started to quote the Geneva Convention. I then asked him, "Viful yuden hust do geharget? (How many Jews did you kill?)" He responded that he was Polish and not German. After I put my rifle to his head he turned over the watch. When the watch needed repair after the war I gave it to my friend Buggy who was studying watchmaking under the G. I. Bill. Unfortunately, that was the last I ever saw of the watch.

On October 24, 1944, we were dug in on the top of a hill. The Germans were positioned on the adjacent hill. We were supposed to move out early in the morning and we were told not to break out our rations. After a few hours our sergeant tried to find out when we were leaving. When he returned, we left our foxholes to find out if we could eat. The Germans spotted us and fired a barrage of mortar shells which included a "screaming mimi," an eight-barreled mortar which ejected shells by a battery-operated mechanism. It was a psychological weapon that scared the hell out of you. It made a whining noise as each shell was ejected. I ran like hell back to my foxhole, but did not make it in time. Shrapnel hit me in the back, both legs, and hand.

Fortunately, the only metal in this mortar shell was the casing. If I were hit with a conventional mortar shell, which had metal fragments inside the shell, they would have picked me up with a shovel. Again, I was lucky. Medics, called litter bearers because their job was to carry the wounded to a triage area, were carrying me down the mountain when we were caught in another barrage. My "hero medics" left me on the exposed path and took cover. Fortunately the shells missed. These medics were new replacements so I excused their behavior. Most of the medics I knew were great soldiers and did a wonderful job.

I was taken to the battalion aid station and then to the evacuation hospital. My cousin, Nat Finkel, was assigned to an evacuation hospital attached to the Third Division. I asked the personnel in the hospital who were treating me to get word to my cousin Nat. I asked that he be told to write a letter to my folks saying that I was slightly wounded in my right hand and that they should disregard the wording in the telegram from the army saying I was "seriously wounded in action." I also asked Buck Hudson, who was slightly wounded from the same shell, to send off a similar letter. Thank God the letters arrived before the telegram.

I was eventually flown back to Rome, Italy, to a general army hospital. I recall the ambulance ride to the airport in France but I do not remember the airplane trip to Italy. I was wounded on October 24, 1944, transferred to the evacuation hospital on October 25, and woke up in the General Hospital in Rome on October 30. I have no idea what transpired in the intervening days.

When I woke up, I had casts on both legs from my toes to my hips. My left tibia and fibula were shattered and had been reattached with a metal plate and four screws. I was also wounded just above the right knee. My right calf had been blown away so a skin graft was transferred from my left thigh to cover the raw area on my right calf. I also had shrapnel in my lower back that required the bandaging of my complete lumbar region. My right hand was wrapped like a boxing glove. I do slightly recall hearing the surgeon say that he may have to amputate my right ring finger. After I regained consciousness, I took inventory of my right hand to make sure all five fingers were accounted for.

When I had to use a bedpan, it took two orderlies to put me on and one to wipe. I had no complaints because I had the million dollar wound. I had all my limbs and I was going home. Everything is relative. I was quite fortunate. The patients on both sides of me each lost a leg. The kid opposite my bed, a tank driver, lost both his legs when his tank blew up. Watching the orderlies carry this young man to the latrine because he could not use the bedpan with only stumps was a pitiful sight.

My morale was good since I was never in much pain. My main goal was to get off my back and sleep on my side. I could not write home myself because of the thick bandages on the fingers of my right hand. I dictated letters to my fellow patients who could write, the nurses, or to my visitors. Unfortunately, I did not always distinguish between my fingers and hand. In one letter I would describe the condition of my fingers and in the next my hand. Naturally, my family was reading between the lines and assumed that I was lying and that my hand was amputated. It was a great day in the Finkel household when I wrote my first letter with the pen tucked between the bandages of my right hand. I did not inform them about my other wounds until I returned to the States.

While I was hospitalized, I was entitled to one and a half rations per meal. This included milk with each serving. I really missed my milk while on the front lines. I was drinking the white stuff with relish.

My big problem was how to have my milk when meat was served. I remedied that dilemma by drinking the milk before eating my meat dish. Old habits and traditions are difficult to forget.

Boredom was not a problem during my hospital stay in Italy. We were bedded down in large open wards and there was always kidding and joking among the guys. I remember one occasion when this good-looking Italian kid from Pittsburgh was always bragging about his sexual prowess. Unfortunately, a minute piece of shrapnel hit him in the groin area and the surgeons had to remove one of his testicles. A couple of the guys jokingly told him to stop discussing his sex life since he would no longer be able to perform. The next day, during the doctor's morning rounds, the kid asked in a stage whisper that carried throughout the ward, "Will I be able to use it again, sir?" The doctor replied, "That is why you have two, soldier." I can still hear his sigh of relief and see the smile on his face.

The ambulatory patients were a tremendous help to those of us who were bedridden. We would warn the slightly injured GIs to be careful if they planned to sneak into town or to the base movie because they were being watched when they left the ward. They never listened and were usually shipped back to their outfits in a day or two.

I spent most of my spare time sleeping or reading. I usually read a mystery book a day. My favorite author was Erle Stanley Gardner who wrote the Perry Mason books.

A month and a half after I was wounded, I finally left Italy on December 11, 1944. I was put on a hospital ship and arrived in Stark General Hospital, Charleston, South Carolina, on Christmas day. I immediately called home. My sister Esther answered and I stupidly mentioned that I was calling from my hospital bed. Of course she immediately asked why I was in bed if I was only wounded in the hand. I finally told my family that I was also wounded in my back and legs.

On December 28, I was sent by train from Charleston to Battey General Hospital in Rome, Georgia. I was very disappointed because I was led to believe that I would be shipped to a hospital closer to home. I was counting on Halloran Hospital, in Staten Island, or Fort Dix, in New Jersey.

My brother-in-law, George Harrison, was the first member of the family to visit me. He was on official business in Atlanta and detoured to Rome, Georgia, to see me. My mother and Esther came to visit me as soon as they could get train reservations. By that time I had the cast off my right leg and the bandages removed from my back. I had a walking cast on my left leg with a rocker on the bottom. By the time Mom and Esther arrived, the shock was not too great because I was able to get around with the help of a cane. My good friend, Bernard Goodman, better known as Buggy, also visited when he was on leave from his Coast Guard stationed in New Orleans.

My fractured ring finger was healing, but it was stiff and joined together with my middle finger. The doctors had to splice the two, grafting some skin from my right thigh to the webbing between my two fingers. The doctors were very excited about the results. They had performed some experimental surgery on me, using a dental mold as the foundation for the transferred skin.

My cast was often changed so the technicians could take x-rays of the fractured tibia and fibula and clean the open wounds. I always reminded them to allow for the bow in my leg when they would put on the new cast. I was often ignored. After the plaster of paris would harden, the cast would cut into my leg. This would necessitate a new cast the next day.

The big day finally arrived when they removed the cast and told me I could go home on furlough. I asked for crutches but was told I could only get a cane. I was informed about my furlough on Friday. I practiced walking in the ward and hallways on Saturday and Sunday and had some therapy on Monday. On Tuesday I officially began my twenty-day furlough.

I took a bus from Rome, Georgia, to Atlanta and picked up a train to New York. I only had about a twenty-degree bend in my knee and wondered how I would manage those few days sitting in coach. I met another G.I. in the train station who was in the same predicament and we received permission from the conductor to load early. Since there was no reserved seating we turned the opposite seats around and extended our legs, taking up four seats for the two of us. Some of the passengers complained, but we figured they owed us.

The train finally arrived in Pennsylvania Station in Manhattan. I was completely exhausted from sitting up during the entire trip and not getting any sleep. I walked downstairs to the subway station and took the IRT to the Pennsylvania Avenue station in Brooklyn. I flagged down a taxi and after a long five-block ride, I finally arrived home. I had been away for about two years.

The folks greeted me with open arms. The tears were really flowing. It was the first time I ever saw Pop cry. Esther said that he broke down at the seder the year before, when he saw the empty chairs that belonged to Allan and me.

Most of the boys were still in active service. Buggy was home on leave from the Coast Guard recuperating from a serious truck accident. Jake Frankel, recovering from pleurisy, was also available. Buggy had his father's car and, with our gasoline ration coupons available, we were all set to live it up.

We decided to go to the Metropolitan Movie Theater in downtown Brooklyn. The lights were practically all on in the balcony and all the young couples were smooching. We looked at each other and left for the Biltmore Dance Hall on Flatbush Avenue. We picked up three girls and left for our Cellar Club on Vermont Avenue. The scene in the car was a comedy routine. Buggy, who lost a kidney in his accident, would stop the car every fifteen minutes to urinate. Jake was coughing his guts out. I would scream if I bent my knee too much.

I started feeling awful during the last week of my furlough. We attended Irving Habib's wedding the Saturday evening before I had to return to the hospital. I told Buggy that I felt bad and that my urine was the color of dark tea. Buggy by this time was a connoisseur of urine because of his kidney problem. He made me fill up a shot glass and I remember him saying, "I have seen specimens in all shades, but not this dark in color."

On Sunday, I started back to Battey General Hospital in Rome, Georgia. When I had to change trains in Washington, D.C., I had to ask a conductor to assist me. I managed to find a taxi after I arrived in Atlanta and he drove me to Rome. After checking in at the hospital, they took one look at me and diagnosed a case of hepatitis. By this time my eyes and skin were the color of ripe bananas. I was immediately transferred from the orthopedic to the medical ward and put on intravenous glucose. There were about fifty of us in the ward receiving intravenous fluids simultaneously three or four times a day. It seemed that almost every GI that was wounded and received blood transfusions came down with hepatitis.

I had a very bad case and was on the critical list for a while. The itching was intolerable. If I cut myself the bile would ooze through the broken skin. At night they would put socks on my feet and gloves on my hands and tape them to my pajamas. It did not help because I would rip off the tape. This period was much worse than lying in bed with casts over my broken bones. I was bedridden for three months before I was transferred back to the orthopedic ward.

Buggy visited me for a few days during my recuperation on his way back to New Orleans. I was taking vitamin pills in massive doses to help restore my health. The number of pills to consume daily were great so they converted the dosage into a drink. Naturally, Buggy had to sample the drink and he came down with a case of diarrhea. Since he was the only sailor in an army town, Buggy had a great time with the women after visiting hours.

I was scheduled to receive another skin graft to cover the depression on my left leg where the tibia and fibula were shattered. After my bout with hepatitis, the doctors decided that it was up to me whether I wanted to endure another operation at that time. They said I could schedule it at a future time if it was still needed. It did not take me very long to tell them that I had enough.

There was a radio program that dedicated songs to GIs that were severely wounded in action. I was selected to make my choice while recuperating from hepatitis. I still had my sense of humor as evidenced by my choice of "One Meatball." My cousin Pearlie heard the announcement and immediately called my folks.

I was finally shipped out to Camp Upton, New York, an orthopedic discharge center. I was stationed there for about a month and received weekend passes. I started dating Dotty, my future wife, during that period. I had met her when my cousin Shirley brought her along to visit me when I was home on furlough. Dot says she was not impressed with me the first time we met. I had a moustache, was thin, pale, and already showing some early effects of my hepatitis. Truthfully, I do not recall our first meeting.

One afternoon, while I was home from Camp Upton on a weekend pass, I was watching the boys play ball in the schoolyard. I noticed this cute girl with my cousins Florence and Muriel who lived across from the school. I naturally went over to my cousins, inquired about their health, and asked Dot out. For our first date, that evening, we went to a movie in downtown Brooklyn and saw *Salome and How She Danced* with Yvonne DeCarlo. We were married after a two-year courtship and lived happily ever after.

I recall that the doctor who mustered me for discharge said, "I have been on duty for three hours and you are the first orthopedic case being discharged for wounds received in action." I was officially discharged from the army on November 16, 1945.

My army medals
Left column (top to bottom): American Campaign medal, Purple Heart, Army
Good Conduct medal, Germany Army of Occupation medal
Middle column: Combat Infantry badge, Army Honor ribbon, New York State
Veterans medal, metal plate from my leg and one screw that did not break
Right column: European–African–Middle Eastern Campaign medal, Bronze Star,
World War II medal, Rifle Marksmanship badge

After the War

By Murray I. Finkel

The war was over. I was finally discharged from the hospital and Army in November 1945 after serving three years in the infantry. I made two invasions, earned four campaign ribbons, and spent more than one year in the hospital. I was concerned about my future. I was still walking with a cane and not fully recovered from my injuries and hepatitis. I had no accounting experience and was wondering who would hire me with my disabilities.

On the brighter side, financially I was doing all right. I was receiving $96 monthly in disability payments, and I signed up for State Unemployment Insurance Benefits, what was better known to veterans as the 52-20 club. These $20 weekly payments could last as long as one year. I therefore decided to take a month or two of vacation before looking for a job. Socially I wanted to catch up for lost time. I was going out with the boys and trying to make some new female contacts. In the interim I was dating Dotty.

City College was having a reunion for the boys coming home from the war. I was looking forward to possibly seeing Sid Koppelman, a good buddy from my regiment. I knew he survived the war, but unfortunately I discovered that when they were loading the trucks to embark on the ships for the trip home, one of the trucks backed up and ran over him. What irony! To survive the war and then get killed in such an outlandish manner.

The big item of discussion at the reunion was that the Internal Revenue Service was hiring agents. I went down to the Bureau for an interview, passed the preliminary examination and was accepted to attend a ten-week extensive tax course. I was temporarily hired as of

January 3, 1946. So much for my vacation and membership in the 52-20 club.

The tax course consisted of an eight-hour school day and about three or four hours of homework and preparation every evening. There were periodic examinations on the specific subject matters, and if you flunked, you were dropped from the course and fired from the job. After the course was completed, there was a detailed, extensive examination period. If you passed, you were put on probation as an Internal Revenue Agent assigned to doing audits in the office or the field. Fortunately, I was assigned to the field. I presume I passed my probation since I worked for the IRS for thirty-five years until my retirement, plus three years Army time, for a total government service of thirty-eight years.

Dotty and I were seeing each other more and more often, started going steady, and then became engaged. I didn't have a car during my courtship, so we spent a lot of time on the busses, subways, and trolley cars. Our dating usually consisted of going to the movies, Ebbets Field to watch the Brooklyn Dodgers play baseball, or Madison Square Garden to watch City College play basketball.

Dotty worked for Randforce, a chain of local movie theaters. Every Sunday we usually had Chinese food on Pitkin Avenue and then went to a freebie at the Stadium Movie Theater or Stone Movie House.

I had Sunday and night game tickets for the Brooklyn Dodger games and season tickets for all the City College basketball games. City College was the only team to win an N.I.T. Invitational and N.C.A.A. Championship in the same year. We also did a lot of socializing with Sonny and Dinah Bernstein, Buggy and Henny Goodman, and Dave and Roz Plaxe.

The first time I met my mother-in-law was quite an eventful occasion. I was still using my cane to get around, and I overheard her whispering to Dotty in Yiddish, "Dew brengst mir aheim ah cripple? (You're bringing me home a cripple?)" That was the start of a wonderful relationship. After that I avoided her like the plague. Actually, avoiding her was not that difficult. My in-laws maintained two apartments: the official residence where Dotty and her parents lived and the second apartment behind the store where my mother-in-law operated a crocheting business. Most of the time, they ate and slept behind the store. I had very few meals at my in-laws'. In fact, I only had dinner there once, on the occasion that the two families met to celebrate our engagement. She made us gefilte fish and tried to be fancy by serving it wrapped in the fish skin. I almost choked on the bones that were in my portion. Fortunately, Dotty had a very good relationship with my folks, and we ate frequently with them. Friday evenings and holidays, we usually dined with my parents.

My in-laws moved to Florida immediately after our wedding, and our relationship improved immediately. It reminds me of the old saying, "I have the best mother-in-law in the country, and thank God she lives there."

After they moved to Florida, she visited us twice for very short periods. The first time was after Dotty gave birth to Shelley in January 1951 at Brooklyn Jewish Hospital in the heart of Bedford Stuyvesant. We were in my car driving to the hospital to visit Dotty and Shelley, and naturally we didn't communicate too much. Out of the clear blue sky she says, "If you hate me so much, why did you marry my daughter?" I politely responded, "I married Dotty not because of you, but in spite of you!" She responded, "Drop me off right here; I refuse to go any further with you." I answered very softly, "Even I wouldn't drop you off in this neighborhood, and especially since it is snowing and freezing outside." We finally arrived at the hospital, and Dotty knew immediately by her mother's expression and the dead silence that we had had another altercation.

The second time she visited us was shortly after we moved into our house in Franklin Square. Like all new neighbors, we used to gather on the front porch and shmooze. Since my mother-in-law was visiting, they assembled at my house. They all noticed immediately our feelings for each other, and she was exceptionally obnoxious that evening. The next day Sid Shapiro, my next-door neighbor, and I pulled almost simultaneously into our driveways. He poked his head out of the car and yelled, "Is your mother-in-law still visiting?" When I nodded in the affirmative, he asked me if I wanted to go to the movies. I said, "Please, as soon as possible." I gulped down the dinner Sid had picked up without noticing it was raining. We arrived at the movies soaking wet, the theater was empty, and the air conditioning was going full blast. If I had come down with pneumonia, it would have definitely been my mother-in-law's fault.

Dotty and I were married on April 17, 1948, at the Hopkinson Manor in Brooklyn. A few weeks prior to our wedding, I was draining through my scar on the leg where a metal plate was inserted to help the healing of my badly fractured tibia. The diagnosis by the VA was osteomyelitis, and it was recommended that the plate be removed. I went to my own orthopedic surgeon for a second opinion. He confirmed the diagnosis and said it should be a simple operation since they would open the original incision and then remove the four screws and plate with a screwdriver. A good carpenter would be able to perform this operation. Since I didn't want to jeopardize my disability, and because of the simple medical procedure supposedly involved, I opted for the operation to be performed at the Veterans Hospital.

A week after the honeymoon, I checked into the Halloran Veterans Hospital on Staten Island. While on the operating table, I was told the whole procedure would take no longer than thirty minutes. I was under anesthesia in excess of three hours and woke up with a cast from my hip to my toes. Two of the screws had broken off into the tibia, and the surgeon had to chip away part of the bone to get enough leverage to pull out the screws.

Dotty used to visit me at Halloran almost every day. Remember, we were newlyweds. Dotty worked in Flatbush. She would walk to the Franklin Avenue Station on the I.R.T. line and take the express to Brooklyn Bridge, and then take the local to South Ferry. She would then board the ferry for a wonderful trip to Staten Island, and then finally a bus to the hospital. The busses were old and dilapidated, and unfortunately they had difficulty climbing the steep hills when the busses were overloaded. This necessitated the passengers to get off and walk to the top of the hill and then reload the bus. If the connections went well, the entire trip was about ninety minutes. The trip home was longer since she had to continue on to the New Lots Avenue Station.

I spent about six weeks at the hospital and received weekend passes during the latter part of my stay. They had to change my cast often to treat the infection and monitor the new breaks in my leg.

While returning to Halloran after one week of my weekend passes, my ward was roped off and the place was jumping with the FBI. The old timer in the adjacent bed to mine, a veteran of World War I, was an alcoholic. He became a patient because he fell off the subway platform and lost his leg to an incoming subway train. It seems that someone smuggled in some cheap wine, and he became drunk. He then defecated in bed and stumped the excrement with the stump of his leg. He developed blood poisoning and died. I don't know the outcome of the investigation.

I eventually healed and was finally discharged from the Veterans' Hospital. Since apartments were not available after the war, we moved in with my parents. The folks lived in a six-room railroad flat on New Lots Avenue in Brooklyn. My sister Esther, her husband Albert, and my newborn niece Bonnie were already boarding in the apartment.

The living room was converted into a bedroom, and the three Kasdens resided there. Mom and Pop were in the master bedroom, and Dotty and I slept in the small room. Our bed filled up the entire room, and the windows faced New Lots Avenue, which was a main street. Before the war, the trolley stopped on our corner. During the war, they converted to busses. When the busses grinded to a stop in front of our house, it felt as if the bus was joining us in our bed.

Since we were newlyweds, we had occasional sex. To get to the bathroom, we had to slide out of the bed because of the confined quarters and walk though the folks' room in the pitch dark. We then continued on through the small inside room and dining room, which was the storage area for the living room furniture, clothing, and everything else that couldn't fit in the bedrooms. It was then on to the bathroom, which had to accommodate six adults and one infant. The beds in the folks' room had wooden footboards. Dotty and I were continuously bruised and black and blue all over.

After approximately three months with the folks, we found a three-room walk-up apartment on the third floor on East 94th Street in East Flatbush. We moved in the fall of 1948. We loved the little place. It was private and all ours.

Shortly after, we purchased our first automobile, which was a gray four-door Pontiac sedan. The dealer was located on 32nd Street and 7th Avenue in Manhattan. I learned to drive in my brother Allan's old Dodge and received my license in 1940. Allan was inducted into the Army in 1941 and sold his Dodge. I didn't drive in the interim, and no way was I going to drive the new Pontiac home from New York on a Friday evening. Aaron Klebanow, one of the boys in my office, offered to drive my car from the dealer to Brooklyn. When we hit the Interboro Parkway, Aaron slid over into the passenger seat, and I took over the driving for the first time in eight years. Traffic was heavy. It was Friday evening, and it was rush hour. I sweated and aged rapidly but finally made it home with the car and myself in one piece respectively.

Pop was on Dotty to quit work from the day we were married. It wasn't proper for a Jewish wife to work. Now that we had our own apartment, it did not take too much additional coaxing by Pop for Dotty to quit her job. She retired at the age of twenty-one.

During the summer of 1949, Dotty spent the season at the folks' new bungalow in South Fallsburg. I made the weekend bull run every Friday night. During that summer, Dotty had a miscarriage and became pregnant again in 1950. The doctor wouldn't allow Dotty to walk up the three flights of stairs more than once a day. The doctor's young assistant would come to our house twice a week and give Dotty sheep's pituitary gland shots to prevent losing the baby. When the folks went up to South Fallsburg for the summer, we moved back into New Lots Avenue again.

A New Generation of Finkels

By Murray I. Finkel

Moving to Queens and Shelley's Birth

The summer was over, and the folks returned from South Fallsburg to New Lots Avenue. We naturally moved back to our walk-up apartment on East 94th Street. Dotty, being pregnant, found it a hardship to walk up the three flights of stairs. We started looking for an elevator apartment and possibly four rooms. Apartments were difficult to find, but fortunately we found a three-room elevator apartment at 88-36 Elmhurst Avenue in Elmhurst, Queens in 1950.

The apartment building was comparatively new, constructed just prior to the war. The building was immaculate, and the Super was strict as far as maintaining the apartment house. The brass doorknobs and accessories were always polished, and the lobby furniture was in wonderful condition. Sitting in front of the building was strictly forbidden. There was a designated area on the side of the building for the baby carriages and chairs.

The location was great. We were twenty minutes from Manhattan and just one local stop from the Roosevelt Avenue station for the E and F express trains. Two blocks north was the Flushing elevated line.

Dotty was in labor, and she was ready for the trip to Brooklyn Jewish Hospital. Since it was January, I rushed down to check that the car would start. I usually checked my shoes before entering the apartment, because the streets were often full of dog shit. I was a little nervous and omitted the procedure this one time. I tracked dog shit all over the house. Dotty would not leave for the hospital until we cleaned up the mess. We were both on our hands and knees scrubbing the carpet and floors until it passed her inspection.

Shelley was born on January 25, 1951. She was a beautiful baby and very good. Our babysitter never saw her when she was not sleeping and asked to be invited to her first birthday party so she could see her awake. The young babysitter was impressed. Because Shelley was such a good child, we were able to take advantage of the proximity to Manhattan. Quite often we would go to the city to see a show or attend a game at Madison Square.

When Shelley was about two, we bought her a purple Princess Ann coat and leggings to match. Perfect strangers often stopped us on the street to comment on how beautiful a child she was. Shelley used to thank them very politely.

My sister-in-law Rosie came to visit with the kids. My nephew Lenny, the oldest, was about eleven. I asked him to drop off the garbage down the incinerator that was on the wall adjacent to our apartment. About one half-hour later, the Super knocked on our door very excited and agitated. He was yelling that no one ever left the garbage in the elevator before and threatened us with eviction if we did it again. The incinerator was to the left of our apartment, and the elevator was open, and he deposited the garbage in the elevator. Living in a private home, Lenny was not familiar with the word "incinerator." It just happened that I cleaned out our mail that morning, and my name was all over the garbage.

Moving to Long Island and the Boys' Births

Shelley was ready for her own bedroom. The choice was a larger apartment or a house. Naturally, Dotty chose the latter. We preferred living near the city, so we limited our search to Valley Stream and the West Hempstead/Franklin Square area. We eventually decided on a house in Franklin Square. It was a basic ranch, three bedrooms and two bathrooms. Our long-range plan was for Pop to build an attached garage, finish the basement, and add a den. Pop eventually did all three.

I commuted to work by the Long Island Railroad and parked the car in Valley Stream, or I drove to the last subway stop at 179th and Hillside

Avenue. I carpooled for a while, but it became too inconvenient, so we purchased a used car for commuting. The area was a young community, and Shelley had many friends. She was almost three-years old, and we were ready for a second child.

Andy was born on May 29, 1954, at North Shore Hospital. The hospital had just opened, and there were only five patients in the maternity ward when Dot delivered. Dorothy Collins, the singer on the TV show *The Hit Parade,* was one of them. After a few days I took Dotty home, but we left Andy in the hospital until the bris that was on the eighth day. The hospital charged us three dollars a day for the interim period. That was a real bargain. The hospital only permitted five people for the circumcision, so we only invited the folks and my sister Esther. We brought Andy home after the bris, and Shelley, our little entrepreneur, was charging a penny for her friends to peek at her new brother through the window.

Andy was a good kid, but there was some excitement in his early years. When he was two-years old, he was on the stepstool holding a metal safe in the shape of a mailbox watching his mother make pancakes on the stove. He fell off the stool and landed on the safe, resulting in a compound fracture of his left arm. We rushed him to the hospital and had his arm set and placed in a cast. While in the cast, he did everything with his right arm. After the cast was removed, he reverted back to his left arm. Once a lefty, always a lefty.

When Andy was about three, he and Shelley were arguing at the kitchen table. I told them that they had to be quiet at the dinner table, and if they wanted to fight, it would have to wait until after dinner was over. They ended up wrestling in the living room after dinner. Shelley, being much bigger at that age, ended up with her knees on Andy's shoulders, which resulted in Andy fracturing his collarbone. His entire upper body was placed in a cast for six weeks. We had to borrow pants from bigger neighbor kids to fit over the cast.

On another occasion, when Andy was about six, he complained about pain when he urinated. Dot rushed him to Dr. King, and he diagnosed the pain as appendicitis. He was rushed to Long Island Jewish for an emergency appendectomy.

When Andy was about seven, our next-door neighbor, Kenny Shapiro, asked to see a new baseball bat Andy had just received for a present. Andy didn't really trust Kenny with his bat, so he stayed pretty close by. Unfortunately, Kenny decided to show Andy the proper way to swing, and the follow-through hit Andy flush in the mouth. He was bleeding profusely, and his baby teeth were falling out. Dotty grabbed a towel, placed it against his mouth, and drove him to the local dentist. Fortunately, the only damage was to his baby teeth. We then traveled to Dr. Blank, our family dentist, who x-rayed his mouth, and the broken teeth were extracted. Dr. Blank told us then that he could tell that Andy would be tall, because the x-rays showed he was going to have big permanent teeth.

Gary was born on May 7, 1957, at Long Island Jewish Hospital. We always wanted three kids at three-year intervals, so we were really lucky. Gary weighed in at eight pounds thirteen ounces. The circumcision was held in a special bris room at the hospital. We had a large turnout, making up for the five we were limited to at Andy's bris. The mohel performed behind a large plate glass partition. He was putting on a big show since we had some pregnant women in the audience. After more than a two-hour wait, the hospital finally released Gary, and we took him home.

We had a wonderful, competent nurse. Mrs. Smith was the same nurse we hired for Andy. Dot was in a mood for Chinese food, so we briefed Mrs. Smith on all the details and listed all the important phone numbers. We came home after an early dinner. Dr. King, our pediatrician and a very meticulous person, was parked in front of the hydrant about five feet into the street. We ran out of the car and saw a path of blood in the house. Dr. King was boiling his instruments in the kitchen. It seems the mohel nicked Gary's penis during the circumcision and didn't inform us. At the hospital, he stopped the bleeding with a type of styptic pencil or something. Now we realized why we waited so long for them to release Gary in the hospital. When Gary wet his diaper, the bleeding had started again. Fortunately, Dr. King controlled the bleeding, and stitches were not required. Fortunately, the nurse was quick to act, Dr. King was available, and Gary was a large baby. Otherwise, Dr. King said we might have lost Gary. The next day, the mohel called inquiring about Gary's health. Dotty gave him hell!

Andy was a very good baby. He was a bit chunky and not too active. We would put him on the front porch, close the gate, and he had a large enclosed playpen. Gary was much more active. When he was six-months old, he was already climbing out of his crib. We added an extension, which doubled the height, and he still climbed out. He would open the refrigerator and empty out the shelves. Once when Gary was ten-months old, we put him out on the gated porch. A few minutes later, the doorbell rang. A woman was holding Gary's hand and asked if the child belonged to us. She found him in the middle of the street. After that, we couldn't leave him on the porch alone and had to watch him constantly.

Little League and Other Sports

I was more impatient than Andy in waiting for his eighth birthday to arrive so he could join Little League. I was frustrated that I could no longer play most sports because of my war injuries. Getting involved with Andy's baseball teams was the closest way for me to be somewhat of a participant. When Andy was young, I would take him and some of his friends to the ball field and teach them the basics of baseball. They improved tremendously, and when they reached eight years of age, they were ready for Little League. I became the manager of Andy's team.

The Franklin Square Athletic Association's little league baseball used a chain system. The chain consisted of the majors, triple A, double A, and single A, which was the eight-year olds. Once a player was assigned to a specific chain, he remained with that chain throughout his Little League career. The manager was usually promoted with his son. The eight-year olds were selected by the single A managers and major league managers of the chain. Saint Catherine of Sienna sponsored the major league team in Andy's chain. All the team uniforms in the chain were green. Andy's eight-year old team was sponsored by Kaufman Carpets.

The players were selected by the draft system. The kids would throw, hit, field, and run and were rated by the managers on a one-to-ten scale. If you selected a number ten, the highest, your next pick would come after all lower numbers were chosen. A running total was kept, and the manager with the lowest total would then pick until the various stages of the draft were complete. I recommended to the board that since the eight-year olds were actually pre-league, there should be a few exceptions in the draft to allow for carpooling to practices and games. Each manager could pick two or three neighborhood kids before the draft started and be responsible for taking them to the ball games. They agreed with me, because at that early age we were basically glorified babysitters. I selected some of the better players that I tutored before the season started.

Because of the special status of the eight-year olds, we moved up the bases and the pitcher's mound. The strike zone was also enlarged in order to make the game more playable. Each player was to play a minimum of three innings, and the pitchers were limited to a certain maximum innings per week. Because of the arithmetic involved, a few players were able to play the whole or most of the game. The best players played the entire game. If an average player played exceptionally well, I rewarded him by allowing him to play more than the minimum in the next game.

The trick in satisfying all the kids was not to show favoritism to your son or the coach's sons. Andy did get the number seven uniform, Mickey Mantle's uniform, as an eight-year old, however. The number nine uniform, Roger Maris' number, was also in high demand that year. It was 1962, and Roger Maris had just broken Babe Ruth's home run record. The best played the most and the worst just the required minimum. The boys wanted to win, and they respected my judgment. In fact, my teams won the pennant all five years that I managed.

We had two sets of helmets: the conventional batting helmets and the base running type that resembled the ones the fighters used. Some of the kids with poor reflexes were required to wear both helmets when they batted. I would stand behind the plate and yell, "Duck!" if I saw a wild pitch thrown.

Andy and I both worked our way up the chain. The double A team was sponsored by Dandy's Daily Delicatessen, and Triple A was sponsored by Bymor Drugs, a name that would not be politically correct today but that no one thought twice about then. When Andy was eleven and twelve, he played and I managed St. Catherine of Sienna, the major league team. As the major league manager, I was also in charge of the whole chain. In part due to coincidence and in part due to my draft exceptions, when they were eight-years old, about half of my team went to Hebrew School at the Jewish Community Center of West Hempstead, which was the sponsor of another major league team. If the kids wore their uniforms to Hebrew School the day of a game, they were released at 5:45 instead of 6 p.m. Games were scheduled to start at 6 p.m., so I arranged for carpools to get them to the game as soon as possible. My trick was to stall for time until the cars arrived. Each manager contributed a new baseball prior to the start of each game. When the umpire asked for the ball, mine was conveniently always in my car. I would pick a slow player to get the ball out of my car in the parking lot. He always had trouble opening the trunk, so naturally I had to go open the car myself. In the interim, the cars usually arrived, and we would be ready to start.

I'm on the top right. Andy is at my front left.

Andy got better each year. He got to pitch on Dandy's Daily Delicatessen. He started one game and was really in a zone. He struck out the three batters in the first inning on nine pitches, but then had to leave to play the trombone in a Polk Street School concert. He never hit a real home run, which meant over one of the Little League fences at Rath Park where the triple A and major league games were played. One game though, he got really close. The first time up, he hit a double that bounced right before the fence in right center. Later in the game he hit a long fly ball to the left, which was rare for Andy who, like most lefties, pulled most balls to right field. This ball was headed over the fence. Unfortunately, the other manager changed left fielders that inning. A big fat kid who couldn't run was replaced by a more agile shorter kid who ran back, reached over the fence, and pulled the ball back into play. The fielder seemed to be the most surprised person at the game. Jeff

Berkowitz, who was an usher in Andy and Sally's wedding fifteen years later, claims he was the left fielder who caught the ball that day.

Gary was three years behind Andy in Little League. Naturally, he was also in my chain. If Gary's games did not coincide with Andy's, I was there. He was one of the better players on the team. Gary was the star pitcher, but he drove Dot crazy when he pitched. Before every pitch, he would scratch his crotch.

Gary was a natural athlete but was not a long-ball hitter. The team was playing in Rath Park. I was sitting in the stands behind the third base dugout and yelled, "Five dollars if you hit a home run!" Sure enough, he hit the ball over the fence, and as he rounded third he tipped his hat with one hand and stuck out his other hand to show me I owed him five dollars.

Little League games were played in the early evenings. At one of the important games in May, the weather was extremely cool. It was a very close and exciting game. At the top of the fifth inning, I noticed my short stop and star player, Arnie Goldstein, was not at his position. I asked Sylvia, his mother, "What happened to Arnie?" She answered, "Forget it, in the excitement of the game Arnie wet his pants, and he's not returning." On another occasion, I noticed that one of my big ballplayers was walking peculiarly. I asked why he was walking that way. He said, "I'm wearing my athletic cup, and it keeps on slipping." I usually had three cups, and I gave two cups to my catchers. The third was usually a size larger, so I gave it to the largest player on the team.

The Franklin Square Athletic Association also had a fall basketball Little League. Gary was interested in playing, so I naturally got involved. I became the coach of Gary's team that consisted of kids in the nine- and ten-year-old bracket. The basketball league consisted of kids in Franklin Square and the adjacent towns. We played by the Nucatola rules (named after a famous NBL referee). The rules were conducive to young players, because they made the games more manageable helped the kids learn the basics. Some of the Nucatola rules were the following:

1. The game was divided into ten periods, and each player had to play a minimum of five periods.
2. To help reduce the mayhem, there was no pressing. The defense had to fall back to the center court line, allowing the offense to bring the ball up and set up a play.
3. Defensive players had to stay within five feet of the men they were guarding. This eliminated double or triple teaming the better players and disregarding the poorer players on the floor.
4. If a player scored sixteen points, the game was stopped and an announcement was made that the player scored out and had to sit out the rest of the game.

Naturally, applause from the crowd followed the announcement. One would think that the player would stop shooting once he came close to the sixteen-point maximum. Actually, it was the contrary. The boys loved the glory and excitement of the game being stopped, their names announced, and running off the floor to the applause of the crowd.

The schedule consisted of Franklin Square games and games against other towns. We had some good players on our team, and we won most of our games. My knowledge of basketball was adequate, but my ability to make proper substitutions was my biggest asset. Since each player was required to play a minimum of five periods, I kept a card chart with ten boxes and a line for each player. I checked off the period each kid played, making sure that I had one or two good players on the court at all times. The coaches who did not have control of the playing time of their individual players were often stuck with too many poor players on the floor near the end of the game. We were often able to run up the score during the last few periods.

Quite a few of the boys played high school and college baseball and basketball. Many have been successful in their business and professional careers. I hope I contributed a little during the time I spent as their coach. To this day, when our paths cross, I get a big, "Hello, Mr. Finkel!"

Gary played freshman basketball at Carey High School. His playing time was very limited, and he realized that for the time and effort he was putting into basketball, he could get more action and satisfaction in some other team sport. He switched to the track team, where he excelled in the dashes and broad jump.

Andy was about fifteen and Gary was about twelve when they were playing one-on-one basketball on the driveway. I was sitting on the front porch reading the newspaper when Gary's body came flying across the driveway. I immediately knew what transpired. Gary was scoring points on his older brother, and Andy was getting frustrated. His fouls were a bit excessive. I pulled Andy to the side for a lecture and discussion. I recommended that he take up tennis and golf and that by the time his brother and friends got involved in these activities, he would be far advanced.

I recommended that we find a golf and tennis camp for Andy to attend that summer, and he agreed with my idea. Sy Rifkind, one of our neighbors, was the director of the Harder Hall golf and tennis camp for teens, which was at an old resort hotel in Sebring, Florida. We made arrangements for Andy to attend the summer session. We also negotiated a great financial deal, where Andy went as a camper-worker. Andy was a sanitation engineer and an elevator operator. His jobs were to run the old fashioned manual elevator during the day a few hours a week and to take out the trash after everyone else went to bed. I recall Mr. Rifkind telling Andy that he had to play golf and tennis every day. That must have been a real tough life at camp.

Andy's eyes were very bad, and we had him fitted with his first contact lenses before he left for Florida. Andy had a wonderful time at camp and came home a remarkably new individual. He improved athletically and socially. From being somewhat of an introvert, he really got involved at high school and made the tennis team. He made the golf team at SUNY Binghamton and was elected captain by his teammates. The golf team had access to Vestal Hills Country Club in Binghamton, where they practiced and played most of their home matches. He went back to Harder Hall as a golf counselor after his freshman year in college. This time his job consisted of playing golf and assisting pros with their golf lessons. Another tough assignment, and this time he got paid for it.

On Sunday when Andy was home from school, he would occasionally join us for golf at Eisenhower Park. Andy sometimes had a temper and would occasionally throw a club after a bad shot. I would then pick up the tossed club and put it in my golf bag. There were times at the end of a round that Andy was playing with two or three clubs.

Gary was perfectly happy playing baseball and basketball. He realized that since the whole family was so golf-oriented, he had better get involved in golf or be a family outcast. He asked for the opportunity to go to Harder Hall. We registered him at camp the summer Andy was a counselor. Gary also was a camper-worker, a sanitary engineer. To this day, Gary plays golf and tennis, but is not as good as his brother. Andy was a late bloomer, and his older brother status has been restored.

Passover at New Lots Ave (mid 1960s)
top: Grandma Bessie and Grandpa Max, Bonnie
middle: Cliff, Shelley
bottom: Andy, Gary

top: Barbara, Grandma in Plato Street dining room
bottom: Grandma Bessie, Grandpa Max, Bonnie, Barry in Plato Street living room

SOUTH FALLSBURG (GOD'S COUNTRY)

By Murray I. Finkel

Bernie Davis, my uncle, originally inherited the property for the Finkel compound on which the homes were built. He was married to Aunt Dora, one of the two Finkel sisters. The other sister was Aunt Ethel who was married to Sam Kobrin. The Davis' already owned a large brick all-year-round house located on Route 42.

Of the Finkel brothers, Max, Harry, and Charlie were carpenters, and Morris was a jack-of-all-trades. Sam Kobrin was a plumber. They were all master craftsmen. Between the five uncles, they completed the entire construction themselves, except for the electrical work, some minor cement pouring, and leveling and clearing the terrain.

The first batch of homes built were those of Julius, Abe, Morris, and Sam. They were located off Route 42 behind Bernie and Dora Davis' house. Eventually a swimming pool was built behind Morris' and Sam's units. The uncles added a bathroom, dressing rooms, and storage areas to the pool area.

The second section of homes was built off Lincoln Road about one-quarter mile off Route 42. Those houses were for Max, Charlie, and Harry and were built up a steep hill from the road. We called this section uptown, and the first section downtown. Years later a fourth house was built uptown for Stan and Pearl Schneider, children of Abe Finkel. In total, after all was completed, we had a community of nine homes.

The uncles supplied the labor, Bernie Davis donated the land, Julius supplied the construction material, and Davis and Warshow contributed the plumbing supplies. The basic structural lumber came from the supply crates that were shipped full of sheets, towels, and other textile products to Premier Textile Company. Because the crates were not uniform in size, the outside sheathing on the houses were of different widths. When it came time to put on the shingles, wedges had to be inserted to level off the siding.

To walk from uptown to downtown, we cleared a path through the woods. An alternative means was driving between the two sections. But bear in mind that only Uncle Bernie, Abe, and Sam drove cars. Unless the cousins were available to drive, walking was the only means of transportation. Fortunately, the path through the woods was much shorter than the drive down Lincoln Road and up Route 42.

No car left New York City for the trip to South Fallsburg empty. My Uncle Morris knew the width of everyone's car, and the crates were cut down to size to fit the trunk and back seat area. If we allowed him, Uncle Morris would load up the top of the car too. I agreed once to load up the top with a so-called light load. Uncle Morris kept saying just one more piece until the entire roof collapsed. We had to use a toilet plunger to pull out the roof.

I believe the original construction started after the war, in 1946. Since the work was only performed in the spring and summer and the uncles were still working their regular jobs, the basic homes were not completed until 1948 or 1949. After that, each uncle worked on his own home, finishing details and always adding to it.

The main topic of conversation among the uncles during the year was South Fallsburg. Pop would salvage lumber, store it in his basement on New Lots Avenue for shipment to the Catskills. Pop was an old-time construction carpenter. On the various construction jobs in Manhattan, the contractors would build a temporary wooden fence around the excavation area. The fences were routinely discarded after the jobs were completed. Pop would take as much of the fence home as he could carry on his back and onto the subway. Then he would carry the load to his basement and cut it down to the width of my car for delivery to the country on my next trip.

Another lumber source was the quonset huts that the government built for the returning veterans on Linden Boulevard as temporary housing. When the government knocked down these units and replaced them with permanent housing, Pop volunteered to help with the demolition and salvaged 2x3's, 2x4's, and plywood. How he got the wood to his house from Linden Boulevard I never asked. He probably shlepped the lumber on his back or loaded it on his hand-made cart.

Pop was always adding to the house. The original construction consisted of a screened porch, which had a large table and television set, and also doubled for our living room. The rest of the house consisted of a large kitchen, three bedrooms, and two bathrooms. Pop later added a fourth bedroom for the grandchildren in the back of the house. You could get to the back bedroom by walking through either of the bedrooms directly behind the kitchen, or through the back door that led to a small hallway near the rear bathroom. Pop also added an open wooden deck at the rear of the house, with a clothesline that was used for drying bathing suits or towels. Pop also dug up an area in the furnace room in the cellar and built an additional shower stall. One weekend, I brought up some old discarded French doors and Pop converted another area in the cellar to a game room for the kids. The rear deck was eventually closed in and converted to a fifth bedroom. There was an open area facing Lincoln Road. Pop terraced the lower level and it became our parking lot. The next upper level was converted to Pop's vegetable garden.

I didn't get my first car until 1949, so Dot and I depended upon others for transportation to South Fallsburg. I usually traveled up with Uncle Abe or Uncle Bernie. Depending where I was working on Friday, I left from Premier Textile on Lower Broadway or was picked up at the approach to the George Washington Bridge.

I recall one trip in particular. Abe was driving and I was in the front passenger seat. Uncle Charlie and Morris were the greatest sleepers imaginable. As soon as the rear doors closed they would fall asleep. Before the Quickway was built, we traveled on the old Route 17 and usually stopped off at the Red Apple Rest to use the facilities. Abe, Morris, and I made use of the bathroom and returned to the car. Uncle Morris fell asleep immediately as usual. When we reached Middletown, miles up the road, I noticed that Uncle Charlie was not in the car. We back-tracked to the restaurant and Uncle Charlie was outside waiting for us. He must have gotten out after we were in the bathroom, walked in through another door, and we missed each other.

After we were married, Dot and my sister Esther spent the entire summer in South Fallsburg. Albert and I would come up on the weekends and for vacations. Later on, when the families expanded, we split the time with the Kasdens. We stayed in July and they stayed in August.

Dot and I learned to play golf at the Flagler Hotel which had a nine-hole executive course. After we learned the basics of the game we moved on to Tarry Brae and Lochmor, which were two beautiful municipal mountain golf courses.

Counting all the uncles, aunts, first and second cousins, during a holiday weekend we probably had about seventy-five Finkels present. We usually had a barbecue at the pool. The young cousins got to know each other and all became great swimmers.

The uncles played pinochle on the lawn; the women schmoozed at the pool or on the porches. The old folks loved being together, talking about the next project and *shepping naches* from their children and grandchildren. All the family names were engraved in the concrete walkway leading to the pool.

For entertainment, we visited the various hotels in the region, ate in the finest restaurants, or spent a restful evening at the movies. The Rivoli Theater was about a half-mile away on Main Street. After the movie, we would usually get a snack at the Popins restaurant down the block. We would also go the movies in Monticello followed by a snack at Kaplans Delicatessen. Babysitting was free, supplied by Mom.

Cutlers Cottages, a bungalow colony on the other side of town, had a wonderful day camp. They supplied transportation and it was conveniently close. At any one time, between twelve and twenty-five Finkel kids attended the camp. They were known as the Finkel mafia. When the boys became older, they, along with some of their cousins, attended Camp Lakota in Wurtsboro. In fact, Gary's three daughters were also campers and junior counselors at the same camp.

After I purchased my Pontiac in 1949, I would leave the city late Friday afternoon and arrive in time for Shabbat dinner. After a Friday night dinner in the early 1960s, my cousin Nat and I decided to hit some golf balls at the driving range. I talked Pop into joining us. I thought that with Pop's experience as a carpenter, with arms as strong as tree trunks and his ability to hit a nail from every angle, it would be interesting to see the results of his hitting a golf ball. Pop walked out of the car with us, but after some second thoughts, said, "Mir darf zein meshugah. (You have to be crazy.)" That was the end of that experiment.

I would normally leave Sunday about 7 p.m. for the return trip to New York. I found the travel very slow and tiresome, so I switched over to leaving early Monday morning. That wasn't much of an improvement because I couldn't function properly at work. I finally decided to take off Mondays, and I left about 6 or 7 in the evening. I got home in time for a good night's sleep and rested up for four days of work in the city. I chopped up my vacation by taking off Mondays, but it was well worth it. It was also great for Mom, because Dot or I was able to take her to do the shopping for the week.

The routine continued for quite a while until the folks became too old for South Fallsburg. We couldn't leave them alone, so occasionally we would take them up for an extended weekend. In fact, one year the family spent Rosh Hashanah in the mountains, and we attended religious services at the temple in town.

Unfortunately, Mom became quite ill and had a series of mini strokes. This required long periods of hospitalization and eventually she passed away. Pop, Albert, and I would make our annual trip to the country to close up the house and check on the unit's condition. After awhile, Pop was in no condition to travel. He spent his final years at the Hebrew home for the Aged in Riverdale and died at the age of 100.

The house was vacant and boarded up during Pop's final years. During one of our summers in the Poconos, Shelley, Andy, and I traveled to South Fallsburg to check on the condition of the house. Andy was always intrigued with Pop's tools so we collected all that was still available. To this day Andy cherishes the collection, especially the old-fashioned manual pieces.

We never discussed selling the house while Pop was still alive. He loved the place so much it would have broken his heart. In fact, none of the South Fallsburg houses were sold until all of the Senior Finkels passed away.

Top: Barbara, Belle, and Dick; Dick and Shelley
Bottom: Shelley and Dick

Top: Bonnie and Shelley; Dick and Shelley
Bottom: Shelley and Dotty; Murray, Shelley, and Dotty

Shelley, Dotty, Grandma Bessie, Cliff, Bonnie

Albert, Cliff, and Esther

Andy, Gary, Dotty

Summer 1958
Top: (left to right) Randy Schneider Segal, Eric Grunin, Marion Grunin Meadow,
Herb Leventon, Aileen Leventon, Andy Finkel, Shelley Finkel Goldstein
Bottom: Gary Finkel, Eric Grunin

Gary and Andy Finkel (showing the size of the fish that got away)

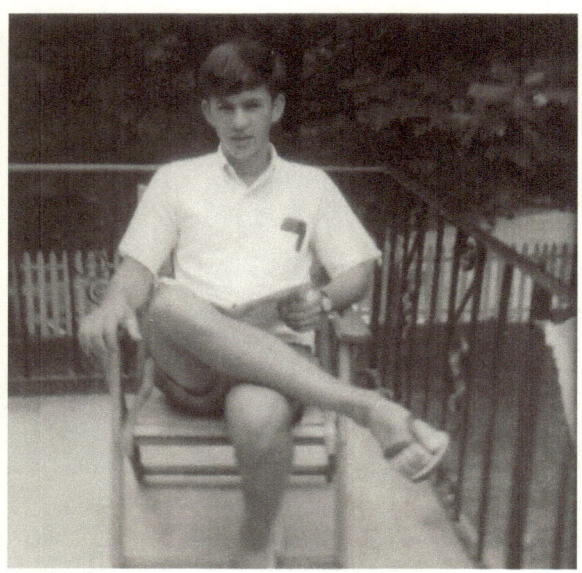

Dick Harrison

Finkel family members' names etched in the concrete on the sidewalk entrance to the pool.

Shelley Finkel Goldstein visiting the bungalows after they were closed for good.

Uptown in 2003, after the property was sold and turned
into a writers retreat by the new owner.

MISCELLANEOUS TID BITS

By Murray I. Finkel

School Lunch

I brown bagged it through junior high school, high school, and college. Lunch consisted of two sandwiches of the previous day's leftovers. The contents were usually hamburger, chicken, salmon croquettes, bologna, or the old reliable cream cheese and jelly. Also included were an apple or banana and a nickel to buy a drink. With all this food that I consumed, I was still very thin. I led a very active life and probably had a high metabolism.

My Boxing Career

When I was a freshman at City College, I entered the boxing intramurals. I wasn't much of a puncher, but I was very fast on my feet, so I used to jab and dance rapidly around the ring. I lost to a senior in the finals. The boxing coach was impressed with my ability and offered me a place on the varsity boxing team. The proviso was that I box at 115 pounds because the boxer at my weight of approximately 120 pounds was the state boxing champ. I said, "Sorry coach, I forged my mother's signature to box in the intramurals, and she would never allow me to join the boxing team. Also, if I lost five additional pounds, I would need pick up and delivery service to get to school."

Big Brothers

Andy had received his driver's license and was earning some extra income cutting lawns. He used my car and lawn mower on the job. Gary wanted a piece of the action, but since he wasn't driving yet, he needed Andy's assistance. Andy offered a proposition to Gary. Andy would drive Gary to and from the customer's house, Gary would cut the lawn and they would then share the fee. Gary complained about what he considered an unfair deal and wanted me to arbitrate. I didn't want to get involved because I might be prejudiced, since I was also a kid brother. I can recall when Allan and I were boys, Mom would allow us to share a Ward's chocolate-covered, vanilla-base, rectangular piece of cake. When Allan started to divide the cake in half, I said, "If you cut I have first choice." Allan replied, "No way. Since I'm the older brother, I cut and pick first." P.S. Gary accepted Andy's offer in sharing the fee.

Gary's Visits to Pop

Gary finally received his driver's license and was available to chauffeur anyone or go anyplace. Thursday evenings, Gary, Doug Friedman, and Little Lip would visit Pop in Bayside and superficially clean his apartment. On the way home the boys would stop off for pizza, and I naturally picked up the tab.

50th Wedding Anniversary

On April 17, 1998, Dot and I celebrated fifty years of marriage. We partied by having a beautiful affair at Buon Gusto, in Roslyn, Long Island, sponsored by the children. All the children and grandchildren, immediate family, cousins, and friends were present. A wonderful time was had by all.

The Army erroneously mailed me a second Purple Heart medal. Prior to the festivities, I donated the medal to Andy, the oldest son. When it came time for the toast he handed the medal to Dot and said, "You earned the Purple Heart for living with Dad for fifty years."

My nephew, Clifford Kasden, wrote the following poem and read it at the party.

A 50th Anniversary for a Golden Twosome

Did you say that life was easy?
Did you say that life was tough?
Lucky couples hit the green in two.
If not you're in the rough.

For fifty years this twosome has been celebrating life.
With Jewish pride, their joy and tears,
Five decades.
Man and wife.

Despite the scars of combat, and a cane to hold his weight.
Murray Finkel met Dot Hassman and were wed in '48.

In the '50s, cousins Shelley, lefty Andy, Gary Scott
Lived on Plato Street in Franklin Square
With parents Murray, Dot.

In the '60s, Uncle Murray coached the little league and then,
He coached basketball and lots of golf, as boys grew into men.
Aunt Dotty decorated every room with flair and style.
Thanksgivings, weekends, Pesach—all her cooking made us smile.

Sunny summers in South Fallsburg—Flagler's fairways moist with dew.
Use a "3-wood" or an "iron." Keep your head down. Follow through.

By the '70s, their children used a college dorm address.
Better find the most deductions.
Good thing Murray's IRS.

Spouses Billy, Sally, Mindy joined the Finkel family.
Seven grandkids, here's the roll call:
Bailey, Jeffrey, Ben, Erica, Dani, Morgan, and Chelsey.

Speaking as their youngest nephew
We look back with pride and love.
Fifty years are something golden.
Zie Gezundt and MAZEL TOV.

Murray, Dotty, and Chelsey Finkel

Thanksgiving 2002

During Thanksgiving, November 2002, Dotty and I celebrated our 75th and 80th birthdays respectively at Sally and Andy's home in Columbia, Maryland. Everyone contributed and prepared a delicious dinner for the immediate family. Since Thanksgiving and Chanukah fell during the same week, we also lit the menora, handed out Chanukah gelt to the children, and ate potato latkes for our evening snack.

(back row) Erica, Ben, Chelsey, Jeff (front row) Dani, Bailey, Morgan

(back row) Ben, Jeff (front row) Erica, Morgan, Murray, Sally, Bailey, Chelsey, Dani, Dotty

MY LIFE: CHAPTER ONE

By Dotty Finkel

When I was a little girl, I would prance around and say, "My Mama came from Minsk and my Papa came from Pinsk." Of course this wasn't really true, because they came from small towns near the big cities.

Papa was a widower with five children: Ellie, Pearl, Annette, Esther, and Harry.

Mama's first husband had died, and she was only married a short time to her second. Papa was her third husband. Mama had four children, Joey, Fanny, Rosie and Ethel (the black sheep). The story Mama told me about her is far-fetched. She said her first husband had a mistress who became pregnant the same time Mama was pregnant. Mama lost her baby, and she said that she took the mistress' baby and brought her up. This is very incongruous, because I look more like Ethel than my other sisters. Ethel must have been very bright, because she slept over once and taught me all the presidents up to Franklin Delano Roosevelt, who was then the President. They come in handy even now when I do crossword puzzles.

I was born on June 20, 1927, at Michael Reese Hospital in Chicago. We lived on S. Springfield Ave. on the West Side. My two sisters and my brothers all swore that I walked when I was six-months old. I was told I had a baby brother named Abbie who died from double pneumonia pleuracy. We lived for a time in LaPorte and Gary, Indiana. When I was four, Mama and I went to New York. We were boarders in someone's apartment for a while. When Papa came from Chicago to live with us, we got our first apartment above the Raymond's Juvenile Furniture Store in Brooklyn on Sutter Avenue. They were German Jews and had no children and were very nice to me. In the back of their store was a backyard with a big tree, and I remember climbing the tree.

I started kindergarten at P.S. 150 on Powell Street. I had a boyfriend, and I was very sad when he moved to Arizona. We would move every year and sometimes six months, because when you took an apartment you got a month's concession, which meant you didn't pay for one month. I went to so many schools I couldn't keep track. I was supposed to skip two times, but we moved, so they put me in the One class. We changed classes every six months. Other times when we moved, I was put in the Three class and then back into the One Class. I'll explain the system we had. Smartest kids were in the One Class, then Three, then Four, and last the Two Class. We even lived in three different apartments in the Bronx, the nicest one being across the street from the Bronx Park Zoo.

We always had boarders in our house. There was a short time when Mama put a perene, which was a comforter filled with feathers, in the bathtub, and I slept there. When we lived on Miller Avenue, we had a very nice elderly man living with us. We were listening to the radio, and Orson Wells' War of the Worlds came on. I was very upset and started to cry. On the program it sounded as though men had come from Mars to take over the Earth. It was very realistic and I was very scared. Our boarder was very nice and consoled me. I'll never forget that incident.

When I was seven-years old, I was playing outside with the Super's daughter and dancing around. A man came up to me and asked if he could talk to my mother. He told Mama that he and his wife had a Dancing School and he thought I was talented, and he wanted to give me a scholarship. Of course Mama said no. When I was a teenager, I had a friend who had a scholarship to that dancing school, and she eventually was in the Corp De Ballet at Radio City. Oh well! What can I say!

One of Mama's friend's sons was having a difficult time finding a job, and he gave me mandolin lessons for a nominal amount. After six months, when my fingertips finally hardened and it was easier to play, he married a very wealthy girl whose father had a leather goods factory, and he went to work for his father-in-law. That was the end of my mandolin lessons.

As far as I can remember, Papa had only one job. He worked in a small factory that manufactured watchbands. Some were leather and others stretchable bracelets. After a while, the boss must have thought highly of Papa, because he gave him a key, and Papa went in early and opened the place. Mama was a very domineering person and always belittled Papa so that he was a real Mr. Milquetoast. He had no say in anything.

My maiden name was Hassman. Papa's Jewish name was Yeshiah. In English it became Sam. He had a brother in Boston whose Jewish name was Shmuel, and when he went through Ellis Island, he was given the name Sam Gassman. So there you have it, two brothers named Sam, one Hassman and one Gassman.

Mama had two younger brothers in Chicago. Uncle Sam was a furrier and Uncle Benny owned a cleaning and tailoring establishment. Mama always spent one dollar for my shoes. Uncle Sam came to visit us and took me to a shoe store on Sutter Avenue and bought me these very sturdy oxfords for five dollars. I must say they never wore out, and I finally outgrew them.

When we went to the local movie, we saw two films, the Movietone News, cartoons, and a serial with a cliffhanger at the end of each serial. We also had usherettes to watch over us. This all cost ten cents. Once a week was "Dish Night." You got a dish and could acquire a whole set this way.

When I was about nine-years old, I started attending Shula. This was a Jewish school where I learned to read and write Yiddish. There was no religion involved, since my family didn't believe in religion, although we did celebrate the Jewish holidays. After I learned to read properly, I would read the Bintel Briev to my mother. This was the Dear Abbey column of that time in the Jewish paper. When my parents moved to Florida and then California, I corresponded with my father in Yiddish.

My brother Ellie from Chicago married a lovely girl named Ann, and they visited many times. Unfortunately, Ellie had a heart attack and died. He was still very young. Ann remarried and came to see us with her new husband. After they left, she sent us a letter saying that her new husband didn't like the idea that she was keeping in touch with her first husband's family, and that we wouldn't be hearing from her again. (Where were you Women's Lib?)

My brother Ellie and his wife Ann

My sister Rosie had married Frankie Vitale and gave birth to Lenny. I was eleven-years old at the time. When he was three-months old, I was visiting them, and Rosie went food shopping and left me with Lenny. He started crying, and when I picked him up he wouldn't stop. I checked to see that there wasn't an open diaper pin and that he didn't need his diaper changed. All of a sudden he became stiff and was turning blue. I thought he was dying. Thankfully Rosie came back and said that he had had a tantrum. What an experience!

When I was twelve, I started babysitting for a couple every Saturday night with an infant who invariably got up with a messy diaper, which I had to change, and I also gave him a bottle. They left at six and returned at twelve. Of course there was only a radio, and I received one dollar.

That same summer, my sister Rosie rented a room in a big old house on Sylvan Lake in the Catskills. She took me with her and I had a ball. There was a communal kitchen and bathroom. That was the summer I learned how to swim. I would swim halfway to a raft, get scared and swim back. After a while it dawned on me that if I could swim halfway there and back, I could make it to the raft. That's how I overcome my fear of the water. I would take out a rowboat into the middle of the lake and enjoy the scenery. That summer I played a lot of ping-pong. In high school I got a letter "P" for ping-pong.

My first date was when I was thirteen. The boy who lived in the apartment above us asked me to go to the movies. After the movie we went into an Ice Cream Parlor and had an ice cream soda with two straws. On the way home he took me around and was getting too chummy, so I very nicely took his hand off my shoulder, and that was my first date.

My brother Joey, who was twenty years older than I was, married a lovely girl named Eva. They moved to the Bronx in a complex called The Coops. It was the first cooperative apartments ever built. We lived next to the last stop of the IRT line, and Joey lived almost at the end of the line in the Bronx. From the time I was ten-years old, I would go there for weekends. I must say that when I was a child, we went all over alone and had no fears. Norma Friedman, whose mother was a friend of Eve's, and I became good friends, and I spent a lot of time at her apartment. She would also come to Brooklyn and spend weekends with me. There was also a very nice group of boys and girls who I befriended. I learned to ride a bicycle on a huge boy's racing bike. There was one boy in particular who seemed to like me and the feeling was mutual. He didn't live in the Coops but all his friends lived there. One day a few of us went to his house. I don't remember why. When I walked in the door and met his mother, I knew that he wasn't Jewish. Since both my sisters had married gentiles, my mother urged me to marry a Jewish boy. That was the end of that puppy love!

When I finished sixth grade, I went to Junior High School 149 where I was in the Rapid Advance program. We did the seventh grade in six months and the eighth grade in six months, skipping a year. After graduation, one of the girls decided to have a party at a Chinese restaurant. Howard Rothman and Gaspare Campanelli both picked me up at my house and escorted me to the party. I felt like the cat's meow because they were two of the brightest boys in the class.

I was dying to go to college but Mama said no, that I had to bring money into the house. I even said that I could go to nursing school and that it wouldn't cost her anything. But the answer was no. When I complained to my sister Rosie and brother Joey, their answer was, "We didn't even go to high school." So I took a commercial course with some minors in Bio.

All through high school, I was in all the theatrical productions. I didn't get to the main building of Thomas Jefferson High School until my junior year, but was in a play in the Annex where I had the lead part as a dean of girls' school. I was fourteen and I wore a black dress, and the teacher put flour in my hair so it looked gray. When I got to the main building, I had the lead in all the plays. When the yearbook came out in my senior year, I was chosen "Best Actress." I went to the senior prom with the president of the senior class, and we led the entourage going into the affair.

I'll digress and go back to when I was twelve-years old. Mama finally bought a house on Hendrix St. There was a store and two apartments above it. In a short time, Mama made an apartment out of the store. My job every Friday was to wash the two flights of steps and the three halls. At this time, Mama opened a Knitting Store on Sutter Ave near Hopkinson. If I wanted to eat dinner, I had to go to the store, which was about a mile away.

Mama didn't knit. She just crocheted. At the time, fascinators were the rage. They were a triangle of crocheted wool in the pineapple stitch with a ruffle around the edge. Mama made them in white; some had gold threads and the others had silver. They were worn on the head. Mama would knock one off in a half-hour and charge a dollar. She sold a great many. After a while, she bought frames and made corday bags, which sold for five dollars.

When I was sixteen, I finally got to know my brother Harry, who was five years older than I was. He was in the Air Corps stationed in Massachusetts and came to see us often. He bought me ice skates and took me to a skating rink and taught me to skate. He took me to Sardi's for dinner. At Sardi's he taught me proper table manners. It was nice having a big brother.

When I was a junior in high school, I got a job at Stern Bros. as a wrapper. I worked on Thursday nights and all day Saturday. The girls I worked with were very friendly and we ate together. One day I said that I wouldn't be in the following Saturday, because it was a Jewish holiday. I think they were all in shock, and from then on I got the cold treatment. Fortunately, shortly afterwards I was the only one in the department who got a promotion to be a cashier in the Jewelry Department. Now that was not easy. We had to figure by hand purchase price, sales tax, and a twenty percent luxury tax. What a difference from today's clerks!

When Shirley moved from Middletown, New York, to Brooklyn when she was fifteen, we met and became good friends. I spent a great deal of time at her house, and her Mom always made me feel very welcome. Many nights I had dinner at their house. When Shirley's younger brother Howard came home from school, he always had a peanut butter and jelly sandwich. I had never had peanut butter and acquired a taste for it. It's still one of my favorite foods.

Howard and me

My closest friends were Shirley, Frances, Evelyn and then Muriel, Florence, and Natalie.

left to right: Natalie, Muriel, Gloria, Florence, me, Shirley

When I was sixteen, I went to Chicago and stayed at my Uncle Benny's house. One evening, my cousin Sonny and two of his friends took me for a ride across the state line into Indiana. All I saw was farmland until all of a sudden there was a block of neon lights. They consisted of bars and nightclubs. We entered one establishment where there was what looked like a boxing ring in the middle and tables all around. The boys had drinks and I probably had a soda. All of a sudden the show began. A girl walked into the ring fully dressed, took off all her clothes, picked them up and walked out. No music, no dancing, nothing. You never saw so many bored faces in all your life. I guess they thought I would be shocked, but I took it in stride. Indiana didn't have very stringent laws at the time.

One of the boys from the Bronx group asked me out on a date. He took me to a jazz club on 52nd Street to see Billie Holliday. She walked in an hour late dragging a gorgeous white fox coat on the floor, but when she sang she was marvelous. Shortly after this date, he was drafted and was sent to the Far East. He wrote to me, and we corresponded. When he came on leave, he brought me a beautiful silk kimono, a fan, and two soapstone figures. I felt that he thought we would be more than friends, but there was no physical attraction on my part, so we remained just friends.

After graduation, my first full-time job was in Manhattan for East Coast Freight Lines. My salary was twenty-five dollars a week, of which I gave my mother ten dollars. Our offices were above the slips for the huge trucks, and the drivers had to back into the slips. All the men sometimes had to take two and three tries to park, but guess what? There was only one lady driver who backed in perfectly every time.

I had trouble walking the steps to the trains and after a year quit my job. My friend Natalie's uncle was the controller for a company in Brooklyn on Bedford Avenue called Randforce Amusement Corp. They owned forty-two movie theatres in Brooklyn and Queens. She told me they were looking for a secretary, and I went for an interview and got the job. Mr. Streimer was the purchasing agent for the company, and I became his secretary. He was a very easygoing guy and a very pleasant boss. After about a year, I was promoted to work for the booking agents. I wrote the list of theatres so many times that I can still rattle them off: Ace, Alba, Alhambra, Ambassador, Benson, Beverly, Biltmore, Capital, Carroll, Claridge, Clinton, Colonial, Commodore, Congress, Culver, Duffield, Embassy, Gem, Ithica, Jewel, Kinema, Lefferts, Marlboro, Marcy, Maspeth, Meserole, Oasis, Parthenon, Rainbow, Ridgewood, Roosevelt, Savoy, Senate, Stadium, Stone, Supreme, Utica. I guess I missed a few!

At Randforce, Anita and I became friends, and we still are today. At least twice a week we would go over to the original Loehmann's on Bedford Avenue, which was two blocks from our office. Wow, the goodies we got! There was one outfit in particular that we both purchased. It was a stunning suit made of a cordlike material, white with a thin line of black. It consisted of a pencil thin skirt and a bolero jacket. The price was ten dollars. We were very well dressed on very little money.

At Randforce, I met Frank Judd. He and his father had the company that installed the ticket machines in all the theaters and if necessary repaired them. He would stop by the office and we would chat. He asked me out. He loved to dance and would take me to the Glen Island Casino in Westchester to dance. I was 5'2" and he was over 6', but we still enjoyed dancing. I guess I stopped seeing him when I met Murray.

I was at Shirley's house on Saturday when she said that her cousin was home on furlough and was leaving tomorrow, and she wanted to see him. She asked me to come along. I said okay, and we went. When I first met Murray, I was not impressed. He was gaunt and had a moustache and long hair.

A few months later, my friend Norma was visiting me for the weekend, and we went over to see Muriel. We were sitting on the bench in front of her house, which was across the street from a schoolyard. All of a sudden this good-looking guy walked across the street and started talking to us. Muriel introduced us and said that he was her cousin Murray. I didn't recognize him at first. He had gained weight, the moustache was gone, and he had a crew cut. After some conversation, he asked me to go out the next night. We went to downtown Brooklyn on the train, and Norma continued on home to the Bronx.

We saw the movie *Salome and How She Danced* with Yvonne DeCarlo. Murray used a cane, and we were permitted to go to the beginning of the line. After the movie, we had sandwiches. Murray only had lettuce and tomato on toast, because he had recently had a bout with yellow jaundice.

When he took me home, my mother was standing on the top of the steps, and she said in Yiddish, "You're bringing home a cripple?" Murray overheard this comment, and he wasn't too thrilled with meeting my mother.

We started dating and after a while went out every other Saturday night. Since I worked for a movie chain, if we went to a local theater I got passes. I met his close friends, Davie, Bernie called Buggy, Sonny,

Benny, and Little Abie. Sonny was engaged to Dinah and would soon marry. Davie was seeing Rozzie. One time when Murray called me I told him I was busy. He wasn't too thrilled, and shortly after was taking me out every Saturday night.

Dinah invited me to their wedding. When I walked in, Murray was surprised, because he didn't know I was coming. We did have a nice time, and he took me home after the wedding. Eventually I saw him Wednesdays, Fridays, Saturdays, and Sundays. We had the same ritual almost every Sunday, a movie and Chinese food on Pitkin Avenue. Now you realize that my friends, Shirley, Muriel, and Florence, were Murray's cousins and soon became mine.

When Murray and I were going out, my mother bought a four-family house on Bristol Street, which was near her store, and we moved there. My parents still slept most of the time behind the store. After a while my mother took her bedroom set and put it into the small bedroom and rented it to a young couple who had just married. I slept on a cot in this large bedroom and told her I thought it was ridiculous. But it was to no avail.

We got engaged in the spring of '47 and planned on marrying in April '48. My mother was constantly threatening us. She's paying for the wedding one day and not paying the next. The whole wedding cost two thousand dollars.

Shortly before the wedding I was sick, probably from nerves, and for the first time in my life, my mother called a doctor who lived on our block. The doctor examined me. He asked my mother to leave the room, and said to me, "You'll be fine as soon as you leave this house." Here I was a virgin and she thought I was pregnant.

Dotty, Barbara, Murray

back row: Bernard (Buggy) Goodman, Phil Leff, Ben (Benny) Golub, Leo Rubin, Harold Siegel, Marty (Mooky) Flam, Sid (Sonny) Bernstein, Herman Rubin, Harold Kobrin, Dave (Davie) Plaxe
front row: Allan Finkel, Shirley Gench, Dotty (Hassman) Finkel, Murray Finkel

My dad and his third wife

top left: Lorraine, Billy, Lenny, and Frankie Vitale
top right: Billy, Lenny, Lorraine, Joe, and Rosie Vitale
bottom left: my brother Joey Keen
bottom right: Mama, Rosie, Shelley, Lenny, and Lorraine

MY LIFE: CHAPTER TWO

By Dotty Finkel

When any of the Finkel cousins got engaged, Uncle Julius, who owned Premier Textile, would give you your trousseau as a gift. We just went down to the store on Broadway and picked out everything we needed. It was wonderful.

Our wedding took place at the Hopkinson Manor, and everyone had a great time until 2 in the morning. Shirley was my maid-of-honor, and Murray's brother Allan was his best man. All his friends were ushers. We spent that night at the New Yorker Hotel in Manhattan. In the morning, we took the train to Miami where we met a very nice couple. They were also on their honeymoon and had gotten married the night before. Their names were Bernice and Sol Schwartz. We were in coach, and Murray and I slept well, but Sol was 6'4" tall, and they were up all night playing cards. They asked us where we were going to stay, and we told them The White House. Murray's sister, Esther, had gotten married the year before and stayed there. Since they had no reservations anywhere, they decided to join us. Since it wasn't the season, we had no trouble getting adjoining rooms and spent the whole honeymoon together.

The first morning, we got into our swimsuits and went down to the pool, even though the sky was overcast. When it got near lunchtime, we went up to shower. When we got out of the shower, we were badly burned. It was so bad that we slept in separate beds that night. The four of us rented a gorgeous white convertible, and Sol chauffeured us around. We saw all the sights—Parrot Jungle, Monkey Jungle, Indian Village, and Dog Track. It was two weeks well spent.

In 1948 it was difficult getting an apartment, and we moved into my in-laws' apartment. They owned a house that consisted of a store on the bottom level and two apartments above the store. It was what was called a "railroad flat," which consisted of six rooms. In the rear, where there was usually a parlor, Murray's sister and her husband Albert resided. Esther was pregnant at the time. In the rear, there was also the kitchen, and off the kitchen, the bathroom. The folks had removed the dining room set and put the living room furniture in what was the dining room. From there you went into a small room with no windows and then into the folks' bedroom. Our bedroom was off the folks' bedroom. It consisted of a three-quarter bed and a dresser practically on top of the bed. Papa had also made a closet, which also took away space. Mama had recently bought a new bedroom set with twin beds, which had head and foot boards. Since we were newlyweds, we had to use the bathroom very often in the middle of the night. We were constantly banging into the footboard.

My father-in-law was very upset because I was still working. He said that a married woman shouldn't work. I said that I would stop when we had our own place.

Just before we were married, Murray found out that he needed some surgery. He had a plate in his leg, and it had become infected. His doctor said that it was a simple operation. They would just open the wound, take out the screws and remove the plate. Because of that diagnosis, he decided to go to a VA hospital. He went to Halloran Hospital on Staten Island. It should have taken about a half-hour. Almost three hours later, they brought him down. He had a cast from his hip to his ankle. It seems two of the screws broke when they tried to take them out, and they had to re-break his leg.

He spent most of the summer in the hospital. I worked in Brooklyn and had to take the train to the Brooklyn Bridge, and then the local to South Ferry. I then boarded the ferry to Staten Island, and then finally a bus to the hospital. The buses were old and dilapidated and couldn't make this big hill. We had to get out and walk up the hill, and then get back on the bus again. Being newlyweds, I went to see him almost every day.

Esther gave birth to Bonnie just after we moved into the folks' house. She was a beautiful baby. I gave Bonnie her first bath because I had plenty of experience taking care of babies.

We finally got our own apartment a few months later. It was on the third floor of an apartment house on East 94th Street in East Flatbush. It was small, but it was ours. Shirley's uncle, who had an upholstery store, made us a beautiful living room set. It was a two-piece sectional couch, club chair, and two ladies' chairs. That's what occasional chairs were called. We got a beautiful bedroom set made of cordovan mahogany with leather inserts at Daniel Jones, a very fine furniture store.

My father-in-law Max was the oldest of eight children. They were, in chronological order, Max, Julius, Harry, Morris, Dora, Charlie, Ethel, and Abe. You've heard of the Kennedy Compound at Hyannisport. Now I'll tell you about the Finkel Compound in South Fallsburg in the Catskill Mountains in New York State. Uncle Bernie, Aunt Dora's husband, was brought up in South Fallsburg, and he inherited a large piece of property. He gave it to the Finkels, and they built houses for their families. Uncle Julius, who owned a large wholesale dry goods store on Broadway in Manhattan, supplied the lumber. Uncle Bernie, who owned a company that sold wholesale plumbing called Davis & Warshaw, supplied the plumbing. Papa, Uncle Harry, and Uncle Charlie were carpenters, and Uncle Sam, Aunt Ethel's husband, was a plumber. Four houses and a swimming pool were built in what we called Downtown. The pool was twenty feet by forty feet with a cabana and overhang. The carpenter brothers built their houses in what we called Uptown, a short walk through the woods from Downtown. Shortly afterwards, Uncle Abie built a house Uptown for his daughter Pearl and her husband Stanley.

Now I'll tell you about my mother-in-law, Bessie. She was a wonderful individual. The mother I never had. I loved her dearly. We spent a great many summers together in the country and never had an argument. Many of the Finkel cousins were envious of me because they all loved Bessie. Esther and I would spend the whole summer together with the folks. When the children were older, we each took a month a piece.

In 1949, I was four-months pregnant and had a miscarriage in the country. We called Uncle Bernie's nephew, who was a doctor in town. He decided to put me in the hospital. He thought we could save the baby. After three excruciating days, I had a D&C. When we got back to the house, I was very despondent. Cousin Sidney happened to be visiting and came in to see me. He was very consoling and made me feel better. Upon returning home, Murray took me to this famous doctor. He was one of the first working on Artificial Insemination. After many tests for both of us, he told us to wait six months before trying again. He gave us the name of an Obstetrician in Flatbush to use.

When I became pregnant and saw the doctor, he said to go down the steps only once a day. He also had a young doctor come three times a week. The poor guy had to walk the three flights of stairs, boil his instruments, and give me a shot of sheep's pituitary gland. For all that he charged me three dollars. Ironically, in speaking to my next-door neighbor years later, she told me that he had been her doctor.

I was four-months pregnant when we got our apartment in Elmhurst. It was a very classy building called the Betsy Ross. There was beautiful furniture and carpeting in the lobby. Even the hallways had carpeting. Our apartment only had one bedroom, but it was huge. There was a large entry foyer and all the rooms were off the foyer. Straight ahead was a dinette and kitchen with a window; to the right off a hall there was the bedroom and bath. The bedroom was twelve by twenty feet. To the left, the living room was the same size. Of course there was an elevator and an incinerator for the garbage. At the time it was a beautiful area. The super would polish this beautiful brass handle on the front door every day.

One of our friends, Lydia, was pregnant. They showed us a beautifully furnished baby's room. Sadly to say, she had a stillborn. When we ordered the baby furniture, the store didn't deliver it until I was in the hospital. I guess you would say that we were superstitious.

When it was time to go to the hospital, Murray, being very nervous, decided to go down to check on the car. Many people in our apartment house had dogs. When he came upstairs for some reason he walked through the whole apartment. There I was on my hands and knees cleaning up the mess before going to the hospital.

Shelley was born on January 25, 1951, at Brooklyn Jewish Hospital. She was a beautiful baby. She weighed 6 lbs. 14 oz. At that time if you had a girl, you stayed in the hospital five days. If you had a boy, you stayed seven days. At that time, breast feeding was not popular. I made formula. First I sterilized the bottles, then I mixed boiling water, carnation milk, and a powder. This was done every night. I had a diaper service, which helped a lot. Ironically, they were very similar to the diapers now but were made of cloth and had snaps instead of Velcro.

I met a couple of very nice girls who also had infants. One of the girls had a nice sitting area behind her house, so we had someplace to take the babies. My apartment house did not allow baby carriages or sitting near the house. We had a routine. At four o'clock we went home, bathed and fed the babies, and they were in bed by six. Shelley was such a good baby. She got up every four hours, had her bottle, and went back to sleep.

We had a sitter most Saturday nights. When we were going to celebrate Shelley's first birthday, the sitter asked if she could come because she had never seen her awake. When Shelley was six-months old, she started standing and walked the day she was ten-months old. People would stop me in the street and admire her. When she was a year old, I was able to go to a wholesale house and bought her a gorgeous winter outfit. It was a boucle coat, velvet leggings, and a bonnet in a grape color. It was so gorgeous that one of my friends who only bought in Saks or Bloomingdales asked for it for her daughter when Shelley outgrew it.

While we were still living in Elmhurst, my sister Pearl's son, Herman, was attending West Point. He came to visit us, and we went to West Point and he showed us around. Herman was going to spend Christmas with us. He called me all excited that one of his friend's fathers, who was a General, had to go to California and was taking the California Cadets with him on the government plane. The next day I heard the report on the radio. The plane had crashed and all on board were dead. Needless to say this was very traumatic for all concerned. He was a terrific young man who wanted to be a lawyer after West Point.

Murray's cousin Leonard Soloway was from Cleveland and lived in Manhattan. When he first came to New York, he was a struggling actor. His parents subsidized him, but by the end of the month, he was broke. He would call Mama and ask if he could come for dinner. She would also slip him some money. But by the time we lived in Elmhurst, he was a Theater Manager on Broadway. We got to see the shows that were at his theater for nothing, usually sitting in the house seats, which were seventh row center. Eventually he was at the Lunt Fontaine Theater. Later on he became a producer and did very well. He had a lovely apartment on Central Park South and a house in the Hamptons. He was married for a short time to a gorgeous gal who was in *South Pacific*. Her name was Anita Gillette, but they got divorced. She moved to Texas and married a millionaire.

After living in Elmhurst for two years, I started looking for a house. Cousins Irving and Tish lived in Forest Hills in a two-storied attached house. The house next door was for sale, and he asked us to buy it. I felt I wanted a detached house with a back yard. I found just what I wanted in Franklin Square. It was a ranch house with three bedrooms and two baths with a center hall. We asked Cousin Irving to see the model. While we were there, Irving met the plumbing contractor who was a good customer of Irving's. Irving immediately checked out the plumbing. He upgraded all our plumbing, gave us a bigger boiler, and beautiful Church toilet seats. This was our housewarming present. Papa built us an attached garage and a den behind the garage. He also made us a gorgeous knotty pine finished basement with another bathroom downstairs. He was so innovative. While they were building our house and hadn't put down the floor in the basement, he made a hole near the washing machine and put in a barrel and a drain on top. When we had a flood, the water just went down the drain. There was even a chest for the children's toys, a beautiful bar, a small sink, and bookcases. We bought a reconditioned upright piano painted white. When Shelley was eight, we started giving her piano lessons.

On May 29, 1954, Andy was born at North Shore Hospital, which was just completed. He was the fourth baby born there. They only allowed five people at his Brith. I left the hospital on the third day and left him at the hospital nursery. I didn't want to be away from Shelley for a whole week. They charged us two dollars per day to keep Andy there. After the Brith, we took him home.

Andy's crib was in the small bedroom off the front porch. A few days later, I saw a bunch of children looking through the window at Andy. I learned that Shelley, who was three-years old, was charging the children a penny a piece to see her new brother. When Andy was a toddler, I would put him on the front porch. We had a gate enclosing the steps. I would put out a bunch of toys and he would play out there.

We joined the Jewish Community Center of West Hempstead when it was in its infancy. I belonged to Sisterhood and also Hadassah. I became active in both organizations. The temple put on some great shows and I danced in them. In Hadassah one year I was chosen "Woman of the Year."

When the children were in Polk Street Public School, we had a group called the "Polk Street Players." It consisted of parents and teachers who put on shows. My neighbor, Mildred Stern, had been a professional singer and played the accordion. She and I worked together performing, and I did the choreography for many shows.

In one show, I played a five-year-old girl just starting school. It was very funny. The girl who played my mother was younger than I was. We had a wonderful principal who was very cooperative. The area where we lived in was all Jewish, but the rest of Franklin Square was Italian and German. There was even a Beer Hall in town where the Bund used to meet. Years later, when our children were in high school, I met the principal, and she said that the school was not the same since we left. Of course I knew what she meant. We had done a lot of good for the school, and that time was over.

When Andy was two-years old, he was sitting on the stepstool watching me cook. He was holding his metal safe, and he fell off the stool. We rushed him to Dr. King, our pediatrician, who was our neighbor. Andy had broken his left arm, and he was a lefty. The minute they took off the cast, he went back to using his left hand.

Andy started wearing glasses when he was seven-years old. When he was sixteen, we got him contact lenses, which really helped. You would never know it today, but Andy was an introvert when he was young. He would never let us know what was bothering him. We gave him a great deal of attention because of it.

Three years after Andy was born, I gave birth to Gary at Long Island Jewish Hospital. He was my biggest baby, weighing 8 lbs. 14 oz. At the Brith, they did not limit the amount of people who could attend, and there was a mob. We were supposed to take Gary home in two hours, but the nurse said that he wasn't ready. After waiting quite a while, we took him home. We had a wonderful nurse named Mrs. Smith. We gave her Dr. King's number and went for Chinese food. When we arrived home, Dr. King's car was in front of our house at the fire hydrant. We ran into the house, and Dr. King was boiling instruments in the kitchen. It seems the Mohl had nicked Gary and had applied a styptic pencil. When Gary urinated, his penis started to bleed. After taking care of Gary, Dr. King said that if he wasn't such a big baby, we would have lost him. When the Mohl called the next day, I let him have it.

Gary was a little devil when he was little. He walked the day he was nine-months old. We would put up the sides on his crib, and he would climb out. Remember me telling you about Andy playing on the front porch? I did the same with Gary. One day someone rang the bell. A woman said to me, "Is this your little boy?" He was ten-months old at the time. She found him in the middle of the street. Beside the wrought-iron fence, there were bushes too, and the porch had two steps before reaching it. Needless to say, that was the end of leaving him alone! I walked into the kitchen one morning, and he was busy emptying the refrigerator and putting everything on the floor. These are just a few examples of Gary as a toddler. But in a few years he was a great kid. No problem at all.

top left: Grandma Bessie and Shelley
top right: Gary
bottom left: Dotty, Andy, and Shelley
bottom right: Andy

Singing "Take Back Your Mink" from Guys and Dolls

top left: Andy's Bar Mitzvah (1967)
top right and bottom left: Gary's Bar Mitzvah (1970)
bottom right: Shelley's high school graduation (1969)

top left: In front of 766 Plato Street (1972)
top right: Andy High School Graduation (1972)
bottom left: Boots on Plato Street porch
bottom right: Gary on his ten-speed bike

left: Andy's graduation from SUNY Binghamton (1976)
right: Gary High School Graduation (1975)

Shelley and Billy's wedding (November 19, 1978)
top row: Cliff Kasden, Barry Tobachnick, Bonnie Kasden Tobachnick, Gary
Finkel, Albert Kasden, Mindy Himmel Finkel, Murray Finkel, Dotty Finkel,
Shelley Finkel Goldstein, Billy Goldstein, Andy Finkel, Sally Jacobson Finkel,
Allan Finkel, Barbara Harrison Judelsohn, Dick Judelsohn, Dick Harrison
middle row: George Harrison, Esther Kasden, Max Finkel, Adele Finkel
front row: Beth Tobachnick Shapiro, David Judelsohn, Amy Judelsohn Gordon

Gary's wedding (August 2, 1981)

In Memorium

By Murray I. Finkel

Kenneth Ian Finkel	September 20, 1967
Bessie Finkel	December 7, 1971
Belle J. Harrison	August 18, 1977
Albert Kasden	February 12, 1985
Max Finkel	July 16, 1986
George J. Harrison	September 12, 1990
Adele Finkel	April 18, 1999
Allan Finkel	August 10, 2003
Esther Kasden	March 11, 2009

Kenneth Ian Finkel

Kenneth Ian Finkel, the only child of Adele and Allan Finkel, was killed in Vietnam on September 20, 1967. The Bronze Star medal was presented posthumously to Corporal Kenneth I. Finkel who "distinguished himself for outstanding meritorious service in connection with military operations against a hostile force in the Republic of Vietnam."

Kenneth was the highest honor graduate of Dalton (Georgia) High School in 1961, and he also graduated with honors from Emory University in Atlanta. In the army, he scored extremely high on the military intelligence examinations and was assigned to army intelligence. He was in military service for approximately fifteen months.

When we received the call that Kenneth was killed, the family was devastated. The body was being shipped by the Army to Long Island for eventual burial in the family plot in Wellwood Cemetery, Pinelawn, New York. Waiting for the body to arrive was rough on all of us. Allan and Adele quickly arrived at our home and we all waited anxiously for the body. After about a week, the casket was delivered to the I. J. Morris funeral parlor and arrangements could finally be made for the burial.

Allan delayed informing the folks about the death until we knew that the body had arrived at I. J. Morris. Allan, Esther, and I drove to New Lots Avenue when it was finally time to inform the folks. Pop was working on the door installing a new lock. Allan asked Pop to sit down since he had some news to tell him. Pop said to wait a few minutes until he finished installing the lock. I think Pop anticipated the bad news. Mom and Pop finally sat down on the couch while Allan told them of the tragic death of Kenneth. We all broke down and cried.

On the way back to Franklin Square, I asked Allan if he ever personally identified Kenneth's body. He said no, but the Army told him it was definitely his son. I said that, "both you and I know the Army makes mistakes," and I drove directly to I. J. Morris. Allan said he wasn't able to go in and make the identification and asked if I would do it. They took me downstairs to where Kenneth was lying in a hermetically sealed, partial see-through casket. I sadly informed Allan that the body was indeed that of Kenneth. He asked me if he looked peaceful and I answered, "Definitely yes."

Pop was upset because there was no way to drape Kenneth with his tallit in the hermetically sealed casket. Our rabbi convinced Pop that under these circumstances it was perfectly proper to drape the tallit on the sealed casket.

After the funeral, Allan and Adele returned to our house where they sat shiva.

Posthumously

Bronze Star Medal Is Presented Finkel

The Bronze Star Medal last night was presented posthumously to Corporal Kenneth I Finkel, formerly of Dalton, who was killed in Vietnam September 20.

Mr. and Mrs. Allan Finkel, parents of the corporal, accepted the medal at their home at 456 Kings Point Court, Chamblee. Major Kenneth Holzer, a c t i n g for the Commanding General of the Third Army, made the presentation.

CPL. FINKEL had b e e n in military service about 15 months, and he was assigned to Army Intelligence. He was the highest honor graduate of Dalton High School in 1961, and he also attended Emory University of Atlanta.

The citation w h i c h accompanied the medal is as follows:

"By direction of the President, the Bronze Star M e d a l (posthumous) is presented to Corporal Kenneth I. F i n k e l RA11956070, United States Army, who distinguished himself for outstandingly meritorious service in connection with military operations against a hostile force in the Republic of Vietnam.

"DURING THE period April 1967 to September 1967, he consistently manifested exemplary professionalism and initiative in obtaining outstanding results. His rapid assessment and solution of numerous problems inherent in a counter-insurgency environment greatly enhanced the allied effectiveness against a determined and aggressive enemy. Despite adversities, he invariably performed his duties in a resolute and efficient manner. Energetically applying his sound judgment and extensive knowledge he has contributed materially to the successful accomp-

lishment of the United States mission in the Republic of Vietnam.

"His loyalty, diligence and devotion to duty were in keeping with the highest tradition of the military service and reflect great credit upon himself and the United States Army."

Bessie Finkel: I Remember Mama

Mom arrived in the United States in 1905 at the age of fifteen. She went to live with her older sister Dvere on Manhattan's Lower East Side. Mom and Pop were married in 1910 and settled in the same neighborhood.

Pop was the oldest in the Finkel family and the first to immigrate to America. As the Finkels started to arrive, the first stop after Ellis Island was Mom and Pop's tenement and later to our house in Brooklyn. At one time or another, all of Pop's brothers and sisters were boarders in our home. Later on, Abram, who was Mom's nephew, and Clara, who was a distant Finkel cousin, also moved in. The last boarder to move in and finally out was "Peril," who was also a distant relation.

As Allan so ably describes Mom's culinary talents, my mouth starts to salivate. Her specialties were *cholent,* carrot *tzimmis,* stuffed breast of veal, *tergachs*—a greasy potato pancake, and *kishke.* I loved the *helzel*—the skin from a chicken's neck stuffed with the same ingredients as *kishke.* There were also other items, too numerous to mention.

I can still recall watching Mom on Friday afternoons cleaning the skin from the *helzel,* sewing up the tears and holes, and then stuffing the delicacy. The net result was a portion of approximately one inch for each of the six of us. It was really delicious. Occasionally I would ponder the benefits of being an only child.

We all knew that Mom was a great cook, but she was a little old fashioned in her preparation. Except for lamb chops, all the cuts of meat—steak, veal, hamburger, etc.—were fried in *shmaltz* (chicken fat) or oil. I didn't have my first broiled meat until I came home from the army. Her first broiler was a round, basic unit with a domed metal cover. Mom's hamburgers were made with egg, onion, matzo meal, and seasoning. I believe this concoction was called *keinkletin.* Once, while she was visiting us and saw Dot prepare hamburger with just chopped meat, onion, and seasoning, she could not comprehend how the meat was able to stay together without all her above-mentioned ingredients.

Mom taught all the women boarders how to cook and bake, helping to Americanize them.

There was a pizza parlor down the street, and Mom loved to eat a few slices and wash it down with a beer. Mom took pride in cooking her kosher chow mein and always asked if it was as good as eating in a Chinese restaurant.

Mom was very proud of her heritage. I remember hearing Mom raise her voice to Pop and saying, "Mein tatte ist geven a malamud. (My father was a teacher, while your father and family were carpenters.)"

Mom was responsible for raising the family and running the household. Pop turned over his paycheck to Mom and kept the minimum amount for carfare and miscellaneous expenses. If we needed money for school or clothes or for our allowances, we went to Mom. Deposits and withdrawals from the bank were also her job. If we had any problems, she was there for us. We were all very close to our mother.

Mom was much more Americanized than Pop. She loved eating in restaurants. She belonged to Hadassah and the ladies auxiliary of the Shul and was active in both of these organizations. She loved the movies and would usually go to the Biltmore on New Lots Avenue on Dish Night with Mrs. Ginsburg, mother of Dr. Jack Ginsburg, our family doctor.

Dotty had an unusually close relationship with Mom. Can you imagine a daughter-in-law getting married and moving in with her mother-in-law? And on top of that, spending the summers with her in South Fallsburg? Dotty's relationship with her mother was very strained. She found the mutual love and respect with Mom that was lacking in the relationship with her own mother. Dotty was usually the one that took Mom to the doctors. Mom also called Dotty to take her shopping, and depended on Dotty for advice and recommendations before making a purchase. Mom considered Dotty her daughter.

On one occasion, Mom was in the hospital for a cataract operation when Dotty received a call that they could not operate because Mom had some blood disorder. Dotty picked her up in the car and brought her back to the house. The next day Mom started a series of tests and it was disclosed that she had chronic leukemia. She eventually had the operation and outlived the eye surgeon and the hematologist. When the hematologist told us that Mom had leukemia, Dot's blood pressure problems began. She was thirty-five-years old at the time.

I went to P.S. 190 until the sixth grade. School was on the other side of New Lots Avenue between Georgia and Sheffield Avenues. New Lots was a busy thoroughfare with the trolley cars running back and forth. Mom could watch me cross the street from the upstairs window if I crossed on the Georgia corner. I was ornery and crossed at the Sheffield corner. I thought I was old enough to not have my mother watch me cross the street.

The folks would often spend weekends with us when we lived in Franklin Square. When I recommended staying another day to avoid the Sunday evening traffic, Mom would reply that she had to be home Monday morning to do the laundry. All her life she did her laundry on Monday. I suppose old habits are difficult to change.

We finally convinced the folks to sell their home in Brooklyn. We found a convenient garden apartment in Bayside, close to the Kasdens.

Mom's health was deteriorating. Her arthritis, high blood pressure, bronchitis, and chronic leukemia were taking a toll. Mom fell in her apartment and cracked a rib. She was bed ridden for quite awhile. During this period she started having mini strokes. After some extended stays in Long Island Jewish Hospital and Syosset Hospital, we were fortunate to have her admitted to Kingsboro Hospital in Brooklyn. Kingsboro was both a hospital and convalescent center.

We visited Mom daily. After awhile she would fall in and out of consciousness. I would hold Mom's hand and I could feel her gently squeezing my fingers. She died on December 7, 1971 at the age of eighty-one. May she rest in peace.

With her older sister Dvere

Belle J. Harrison

Belle was born on November 17, 1910, and lived at 285 Madison Street on the Lower East Side of Manhattan until August 1923, when Pop purchased a house at 330 New Lots Avenue in the East New York section of Brooklyn. Belle enjoyed the finer things in life and resented that she could not live in Flatbush, a more prestigious part of the borough. She was always pleading with Pop to move to Flatbush, but to no avail. Belle finally moved to Flatbush when she married George, and she furnished a beautiful apartment.

Belle was the first Finkel to go to college and received a degree in education. We were all very proud of her accomplishments, especially Pop. Unfortunately, she graduated in the height of the depression, and she struggled to get various teaching positions.

I recall Belle having beautiful pictures of exotic birds painted on a window shade like posters that she used as a teaching aid in the classroom. When I was taking nature studies as a student, I volunteered to loan these posters to my class. My teacher was very appreciative. Shortly after, all the teachers who were teaching nature studies were contacting me to borrow the posters. I felt very important.

Belle was a very good-natured individual. She taught Esther and the younger Finkel female cousins the proper etiquette—how to dress, shop, etc. She taught them how to eat properly and order in restaurants. She also familiarized them with Chinese food. She took them to the movies in downtown Brooklyn and occasionally to Broadway. Naturally, I was also a recipient of these finer things.

Their first child, Barbara, was born in Brooklyn. Then George started working for the Anti-Defamation League of B'nai Brith and they moved to Atlanta in 1945. Dot and I visited them when we became engaged. We became familiar with barbecued spare ribs during this period. We were also in Atlanta when they opened the first Chinese restaurant. The owner was Chinese, the waitresses were white, and the busboys were black.

George was later transferred to Buffalo, New York, where their second child, Dick, was born. After a long stay in Buffalo, George changed jobs for one with the New York State Department of Intercultural Relations and they moved to Albany, New York.

During Belle's adult career, she remained in teaching. Unfortunately, she never lived long enough to retire. She died in 1977 at the age of 66 after a long bout with a malignant brain tumor.

Albert Kasden

Albert Kasden was born on April 26, 1909, on the Lower East Side and then moved to the Brownsville section of Brooklyn. His father died when he was three-years old. To make a living, his mother operated a candy store. Albert was the youngest of eleven children. He was very close to his mother and took care of her until the day she died. Al maintained a solid relationship with sisters Sophie and Edna and brother Mickey, his surviving family.

Albert graduated from the Savage College of Physical Education, a division of New York University, where he won a gold medal in soccer. He continued on for his Masters in Social Work at New York University. He completed his education at the height of the Depression and worked for the NYC Department of Welfare for thirty-five years until his retirement. He was one of the first certified social workers in the state of New York.

Al was in an Army infantry unit during World War II. There he was, one of the first to witness the horror of the remains of Auschwitz. After the war he returned to the Department of Welfare where he met his wife Esther. They were married in 1947 and moved in with Mom and Pop on New Lots Avenue where their daughter Bonita was born.

Dotty and I were married in 1948 and also moved in with my parents. We also shared living quarters in the family home in South Fallsburg. While living together, I found out that Albert was a great guy.

Albert was a very conservative individual. I encouraged him to buy a cooperative in Bayside, Queens, convincing him that he earned enough money to carry a mortgage and support a family. I also taught Al how to drive using my car and explained to him that he was now ready to purchase one of his own. He took my advice.

We played lots of golf in South Fallsburg. Being a natural athlete, Al's game quickly improved. He became a real golf nut. He also always made himself available to join Pop and me in closing the Fallsburg house after the summer season.

Albert died on February 12, 1985, after a short bout with pancreatic cancer. His son Clifford wrote the following beautiful poem for his dad shortly before Al passed away. The poem, along with Cliff's recollection of his dad's war experiences follow.

A Poem for a Nice Guy
By Clifford A. Kasden

In the dawn of the century we now share
Came a group of immigrants, their pockets bare.
The Star of David was their common pride
As they huddled together on the Lower East Side.

A woman among them, eleven children she bore,
Played in the rear of her candy store.
Her youngest son, Al, she cared for tenderly
And called him *mein shaima tattele Allie.*

When he was just three, his own father died,
That relationship ended though barely tried.
But his brothers and sisters taught him life's joys.
Hymie, Mickey, Jack, Al were the Kasden boys.

His sisters Shifra and Edna too
Watched with care as the young man grew.
He was always good to his home and faith,
And treasured them both as a sacred place.

The Depression hit hard and dashed his plans,
But he never was bitter, never less a man.
The silver lining he knew was there,
While some screamed with anger, he didn't care.

There was something about him, an inner peace,
That was always with him, through the cruelest grief.
His motto for life has never let him down—
There's always a smile under every frown.

He chose a career watching over the poor.
Life's wretched and lonely knocked on his door.
It was no surprise that his Master's degree
In social work he accepted proudly.

When the Second World War took him from our shores
Along with his countrymen he witnessed in horror
The remains of Aushwitz, the tortures unknown
That our people endured through no fault of their own.

Although he feared for the future of life,
He looked for that cloud with the silver glow.
He came home to New York and took a wife.
Almost forty years now these two still learn and grow.

He had cared for his mother for many years.
When she passed away, still behind the tears
He knew that the future and life must endure,
So, two children his beloved wife, Esther, bore.

Through the best of times and the worst of hell,
He has smiled through it all and now I must tell,
That the greatest boast I have ever had
Is that I get to call him my Dad.

The golden rule has a new point of view,
Do unto others before they do unto you.
While terror is common, and violence and fear,
Expectations are poor for a calm, peaceful year.

Maybe a change will be needed to stop it,
To make them all say that bomb we can't drop it.
The solution is simpler than it has ever been—
Give us more men like Al Kasden.

Miracle After the Bulge
By Clifford A. Kasden

Al Kasden, my father, was a Brooklyn boy who could slam a killer to the wall with the best of them. That is, when he played handball at Betsy Head Park during the Depression. When he entered the 102nd Infantry Division, 407th Service Company, he used his hands and trigger finger in a slightly different fashion. With the "hunt and peck" method, he won a Bronze Star as company clerk from November 30, 1944, through May 8, 1945.

Like other Jewish servicemen, he felt the pain of anti-Semitism. His best friend, Carmine, was an Italian Catholic from Brooklyn. They had too much in common from the streets of New York to waste time on prejudice. They both relied on everyday luck to stay alive. When the Nazis by-passed their outfit during the Battle of the Bulge, they both thanked God for the miracle.

A more terrible twist of fate occurred when the hostilities ceased in the European theater. As their company began loading trucks for the next deployment, their sergeant began choosing seats for the men. Knowing that Al and Carmine were best friends, he deliberately assigned them to different trucks. He had always resented them. Tragically, Carmine's truck overturned and he was killed. I can still hear my dad telling me how life would have been different if the truck had not overturned, or if his truck had been the one to crash.

Another miracle occurred in 1955 when he was able to move his family to one of only two veterans' coops built in New York. These developments provided safe, secure, and affordable housing for veterans only.

When my dad passed away on Lincoln's birthday in 1985, he was offered a veteran's honor guard. With the guns of war long silenced, a man's religion was a point of honor, not scorn.

Max Finkel

Pop was born on December 28, 1885, went AWOL from the Russian Army, and arrived in America in 1905. Mom and Pop were married in 1910 and settled on Madison Street on the Lower East Side of Manhattan. Pop lived to celebrate his 100th birthday. He died on July 16, 1986, at the Hebrew Home for the Aged in Riverdale, New York.

For Pop's background and history, see Allan's chapter *Memoirs* and my chapter entitled *Stories and Anecdotes of My Father*. His grandson, Clifford Kasden, eulogized Pop at the funeral service with the following beautiful poem.

Building Again, A Remembrance of Max Finkel

When men must choose the life they lead—
Their wife, their home, their lands.
Some use their strength of will and mind
And the power in their hands.

Then tyranny in Russia drove Max to America's door
He brought along a hammer, some nails, and a sturdy saw.
A carpenter has more to do than shaping handsome wood.
He shapes a life for his family in a way that's right and good.

His love of G-d helped him in his tasks,
His duty as a Jew was sure.
You work and pray, do whatever G-d asks
So your people and faith endure.

With all these tools in his steady grasp
Max built not just homes, but a life.
Bessie helped him build and carry out his tasks
As a caring, devoted wife.

Max's brothers and sisters with their own special tools
Were busy building too.
They fashioned their lives with a sense of pride
And helped as they worked and grew.

In the 1940's, the world was fiercely tearing itself down.
And what Max built within him he now had to send to horrible
battlegrounds.
His strength of soul was in his children's flesh while they fought day-
to-day to survive.
It was the strength built inside them that kept his sons Murray and
Allan alive.

His daughters, Belle and Esther, were relieved when the war was at
its end.
And now it was time for Max to start building again.
In the Catskills, they went and bought some land.
A group of houses were built by their own hand.
These homes were built to be shared and used by the whole family.
And for many summery years, that's the way it was to be.

Every relative of every age spent many sunny days
Enjoying the pool and cool shady trees, escaping New York's
oppressive haze.
I know I'm not alone in looking back fondly,
Those pleasant, carefree summer hours are a beautiful memory.

While Max was building happy thoughts for us,
He could not escape so much sadness.
His wife, his grandson, his daughter, his son-in-law, his brothers have
passed away.
For some reason, G-d wanted Max to stay.

Last winter brought a celebration.
A century of living was grandpa's feat.
All the relatives joined without hesitation.
A centennial of his own was complete.

After more than one hundred years, dear Grandpa, you've finished
what you began.
You've been stronger than the tallest oak and I'm proud to be part of
the clan.
I know with Bessie by your side—
You're busy building again.
We may not use hammers and our collars may not be blue,
But your children, grandchildren, and great grandchildren are busy
building too.
You've left behind your own artisans who'll keep doing the building
for you!

back row: Morris Finkel, Ethel Finkel Kobrin
front row: Max Finkel, Harry Finkel

back row: Gary, Cliff, Billy, Philip Bushey, Andy
middle row: Barry, Bonnie, Shelley, Dick, Barbara, Sally
front row: Grandpa Max

back row: Amy (holding Erica), David (holding Ben), Beth, Neill Perri, Phillip Perri
front row: Bailey, Jeff, Brian, Grandpa Max

George J. Harrison

George was born on January 5, 1908, on the Lower East Side of Manhattan and his family moved to Brooklyn. George, a poor Jewish boy, somehow received a scholarship to Wesleyan University, in Middletown, Connecticut, a very prestigious school. In our day, this opportunity was rarely available. If we wanted to attend college we went to City College in Manhattan or to Brooklyn College. Both were tuition-free. George eventually received his Masters degree from Columbia University.

George graduated during the Depression and was fortunate to get a civil service job as a probation officer with New York State. He married Belle on June 29, 1941, at the Brooklyn Jewish Center on Eastern Parkway. It was the hottest day of the year, and the air conditioning broke down.

George was the first member of the family to visit me after I was wounded. He was on official business in Atlanta and detoured to Battery General Army Hospital in Rome, Georgia, to see me.

Shortly after, George changed jobs and worked for the Anti-Defamation League of B'nai Brith in Atlanta. After a few years he was transferred to the Buffalo, New York office and the family relocated. George's next move was returning to the New York state government working for the Department of Intercultural Relations in Albany. He retired after Belle was diagnosed with cancer so he could take care of her full time.

After Belle died, George rented an apartment for the winter season in Palm Greens, Delray Beach, Florida. We owned a condominium in Palm Greens and after a few years of renting, George eventually bought a unit in our development.

George loved Florida and was physically active, playing tennis and golf. We socialized, dined together very often, and had dinner at our house on holidays and other special occasions. He was a great guy.

He died on September 12, 1990, at the age of eighty-two.

Adele Finkel

Adele was born on November 12, 1922, and lived in the Brownsville section of Brooklyn. She attended Tilden High School and graduated from Brooklyn College as a science major.

Adele met Allan while attending college and was married in 1942 at Camp Lee, Virginia. Allan received his army commission there and was then shipped out to Europe. After Allan left for oversees, Adele returned to her folks' on Legion Street, waiting for the war to end.

Kenneth was born in 1943 in her folks' house, because no apartments were available. After Allan was discharged, he moved in with Adele and Kenneth. Allan was working for Premier Textile, a Finkel family business on Lower Broadway in Manhattan, when the opportunity arose to run a chenille plant in Cartersville, Georgia. After awhile, Allan changed jobs and switched over to managing a large carpet mill in Dalton, Georgia.

Adele was a devoted wife and mother and active in the temple. She was a long-term Gray Lady, associated with the Red Cross at the Hamilton Medical Center in Dalton. Adele also taught elementary school for a while, and Kenneth was in her class. He was a perfect "A" student throughout his public school career. Adele gave him a ninety-nine mark because she said no student is perfect. All the other teachers graded him 100.

Adele was a *bala buster* (good housekeeper). Her house was always spotless. It was an experience to watch her change the old-fashioned bed sheets. She picked up the mattress half way until the sheets were tucked in so tight that you could drop a coin on the bed and see it bounce.

When Adele died on April 19, 1999, there was a graveside service at Wellwood Cemetery in Pinelawn, New York. Allan performed the beautiful service, and Adele was buried next to Kenneth. After Allan returned to Dalton, there was a memorial service honoring Adele.

Allan Finkel

Allan was born on the Lower East Side of Manhattan on December 30, 1917. The family moved to Brooklyn, where Allan lived until he was drafted into the Service.

Allan's religious training was at the New Lots Talmud Torah, where he was a brilliant student. He belonged to Young Israel and was usually the cantor at the Saturday and holiday religious services. He was selected because he had a beautiful voice. He sang with the most prestigious choirs in New York City. At weddings he sang "Oh Promise Me," for which he received the staggering sum of fifty cents.

Allan attended Thomas Jefferson High School and graduated from New York University. In 1941, he was drafted into the Air Force and was stationed at Mitchell Field, Long Island. He was home on a weekend pass when Pearl Harbor was bombed and all service men were required to return to their bases immediately. Adele's father had a car, and I joined them in driving Allan back to Mitchell Field. There was no Southern Parkway back then, and we drove back on Linden Boulevard. It was a long trip.

Allan applied for Officer's Candidate School and was accepted. He received his Commission at Fort Lee, Virginia, in the Quartermasters' Branch. He married Adele and eventually shipped out for Europe. After the war in Europe ended, his outfit transferred to the Pacific.

Allan had two war stories he liked to tell. The first was the time a bomb came through the roof of the supply warehouse he managed during the Battle of the Bulge. The bomb caused huge cans of tomato ketchup to fall from the shelves onto him, knocking him to the ground. He stood up with red ketchup stains all over him, shocking the men who found him. They thought he was covered with blood. The second war story involved Allan's indirect conversation with General Dwight Eisenhower. The general never spoke directly with enlisted men. However, speaking through another man, Eisenhower questioned Allan, a supply officer, as to why he had sent a group of men stale bread. Allan explained that the limited resources in the region left him with few local bakers to use for serving the Army's needs. In 1945, Allan was discharged from the Army with the rank of Captain.

When Allan left active duty, he was told his medals would automatically follow. Fifty-three years later Allan called the Georgia State Veterans Administration inquiring about his medals. They told him not to hold his breath, but the medals eventually arrived. They included the Asiatic-Pacific Campaign Medal, the European–African–Middle Eastern Campaign Medal, the American Defense Service Medal, the American Campaign Medal, the World War II Victory Medal, the Good Conduct Medal, and the Honorable Service Lapel Button.

Allan took a job at Premier Textile Company, a family business on Lower Broadway in Manhattan. In 1947, an opportunity arose to run a chenille plant in Cartersville, Georgia. After a few years, he upgraded his career and switched over to managing various large carpet mills in Dalton, Georgia.

Allan was extremely active in the temple. He served as President for a number of terms and was the unpaid cantor in excess of fifty years. He was the editor of the temple's paper and coordinated various other temple activities. In 2001, at the age of eighty-three, Allan celebrated his second Bar Mitzvah at the temple. Almost the entire membership came for the service and party that evening. His sister Esther and Adele's brother-in-law Frankie took part in the celebration.

Allan was also active in the United Jewish Appeal. A tribute letter from the National UJA office stated the following:

> Allan Finkel has never wavered from his identity as a committed and concerned Jew and a decent, thoughtful human being. He has adhered to the principle of *tzedukah,* making him an example in his community and the UJA Network Campaign. Allan has made us a mountain here in Dalton. His acts of loving kindness, his devotion to his congregation, his tireless work on behalf of the UJA has elevated all of us. He has made Dalton a better community.

Allan and Adele were both volunteers at the Hamilton Medical Center in Dalton. Together, they served in excess of fifty years at the hospital. Allan was also on the National Board of ORT.

Dotty and I believe that it was *beshert* (destined) that we were able to spend Allan's last weekend with him. We arrived in Dalton on Friday morning and had lunch and dinner with Allan. We then went to the temple where Allan was scheduled to conduct Friday night services. After walking about ten steps into the sanctuary, Allan was completely exhausted. I suggested that we go back to his apartment at the assisted living center so he could lie down and rest. He said no, that he would be ok shortly, and that he had an obligation to the congregation to conduct the service. After sitting about fifteen minutes, he said he felt better and walked to the *bimah*. He sat on a high step stool and commenced the service. Because the Rabbi was away, he did her portion in addition to singing the cantor's portion. The service lasted about an hour, and Allan's voice was strong and beautiful. He said he felt fine and we participated in the Oneg Shabbat. On the way home, he said he still felt ok and we stopped off at K-Mart to make a fast purchase.

Saturday morning, we spoke with Allan on the phone and he said that he felt fine. I recommended that he have lunch at the assisted living center, take a nap, and rest up for our dinner engagement. He said, "No way," and that he was "thrilled we were visiting," and insisted that we have lunch together. When we went to pick him up, he was still undressed. He said that he had felt a little exhausted so he took a nap, but that now he was ready for lunch.

In the evening, we went to an elegant restaurant and had an excellent meal. We were reminiscing about old times and enjoyed ourselves immensely. We dropped Allan off at his apartment, but he insisted that we sit on the porch for a while since the evening was so beautiful. We shmoozed for a while, and Allan was excited about his approaching Sunday dinner appointment in Chattanooga with his friends Bones and Jessica Boring.

Sunday morning we received the call from Bones that Allan had died. When he did not show up for breakfast, the staff at the assisted living center checked on him and found him on the floor. He had already expired. When we got to the apartment, Allan was still lying on the floor. He apparently had been resting on the couch, had a heart attack, and fell over.

Allan and Adele had a rough time in their later years. They never recovered from the devastating news of Kenneth's death in Vietnam. Allan never felt that well after his second bypass operation, and Adele was suffering from a heart condition and arthritis. Allan felt depressed and alone after Adele died.

Allan always felt that when the time came, Adele and he would be buried on either side of Kenneth, and they would be reunited once again. The time finally came. May they rest in peace.

Esther Kasden

Esther was born on the Lower East Side of Manhattan on October 11, 1913. She was very smart and skipped grades five times in public school. When I was in the army, Esther was my main contact with the family, and she and mom rushed to visit me in Georgia when I returned to the states. She was happily married to Albert for thirty-eight years and was a loving mother to her children Bonnie and Cliff. Her four grandchildren loved her greatly. She was also very active in the Bayside Jewish community and a life-long member of Hadassah. Esther was very independent, living to the end in her Bayside co-op apartment that she and Albert bought in the 1950s. Her son Cliff and her grandchildren Beth and Brian presented wonderful eulogies at her funeral. The eulogies follow.

"A Penny in the Pushka"
Remembering Mom—Esther Kasden
By her son, Cliff

You only get one mother
That's the way that things are done.
A bond that's like no other
With a daughter and a son.

Your brothers, sister, cousins
In a tight knit family.
Finkels by the dozens
Are the roots of a family tree.

Mama you were very smart
You skipped some grades at school.
Education was the place to start
To learn the golden rule.

With Dad you shared so many years
Your lifelong friends could tell.
You're no one's fool, no thoughtless tears
So strong but kind as well.

Remember erev shabbos
Just before you'd bench the licht
A calming glow around us
Evil couldn't contradict.

Troubled nights? So many.
We were worried, we were sick
In that pushka went a penny
And that always did the trick.

A pushka coin's a token
It's a gift to G-d above
That loyal bond, unspoken
Means a vow of strength and love.

For many years on Friday nights
We counted on those prayers.
Mom you were a noble sight
To ease our doubts and fears.

Today that tin box weighs a ton
Those pennies sing their song.
For mama, grand, great-grandma
Tenacious, wise and strong.

So, rest now, mom
You've earned it.
There's just one more thing to do.
In that pushka up in heaven
Please, a penny in that one too!

Eulogy for Esther
By Beth Shapiro

I have this blanket that I sleep with every night. It was crocheted by my grandmother when she was in her eighties. The stitching is perfect. The material is kind of coarse. You know the blanket; you all have one, or two or three. They are a little scratchy, but when you snuggle up under one of Grandma's comforters, you can feel the love.

My grandmother was not a publicly emotional woman. So I am a little bit confused about the demeanor proper for her funeral. Do you cry? Do you not cry? Since, as Grandma would say, "Crying doesn't change anything." Is it worth it? If she were here today, she would probably tell us, "I was ninety-five. I lived a good long life and I died in my bed. Enough is enough."

And if I were here with her, I would tell her, "Come on, Grandma, we all love you. Speaking for myself, I would like to say that you have been a role model for me in so many ways. I will miss you more than you know. I understand intellectually that this world is but an illusion and your soul is in heaven with G-d and Grandpa and all of the people that a woman who lives to be ninety-five loses in a life. But, I remain in this illusion and I will never again see you, hold you, or talk to you. And I'm really going to miss you. So, with all due respect, regardless of what anyone else does, I'm going to cry."

And then, she would look at me and say, "If that is what you have to do, go ahead, I'm not stopping you."

Because that was my Esther Finkel Kasden. She always showed me the flaw in my plan—whatever that plan was—but once I was set on it, she always supported it, without question and without judgment.

She was a constant in my life—like the sun or the moon. In my life, whenever I needed anything, my grandmother, in her prickly way, was there for me. Grandma filled me with a love of stories and a love of learning. She taught me that you don't have to live a fancy life to be happy and you don't ever have to do anything to impress anybody. She taught me that if you do what is right—even when it is hard—and live each day as it comes—even when it is hard—good will come to you.

For the last several years, every time I have left my grandmother's presence, she has told me, "Have a good life," as though she thought that perhaps it was the last time she would see me. Last week, when I told Grandma I was going back to Israel, she would not say "goodbye." Instead she told me that she loves Israel and she and my Grandfather would soon come to visit me there. I believe that they will. Please know, Grandma, that you and Grandpa are always welcome to come visit us—just know that when we want to keep a secret, we might start speaking in Hebrew.

Eulogy for Esther
By Brian Tobachnick

My Grandma Esther has always been a big part of my life. A constant figure in everything I have every known. A constant teacher, teaching me the importance of earning what you have, fighting for what you want, and never letting me forget the value of an education.

A constant companion, playing games like Connect 4, Rummy-O, Crazy 8's, Scrabble, Go Fish, Gin Rummy, and so many other card and board games; having sleepovers on the pull-out sofa in my parents' living room, talking for hours in the dark before going to sleep, and playing word games in the morning before getting out of bed; telling me stories about her youth, about growing up, about meeting my Grandpa Allie, in such great detail, it was like I was there; taking me to Broadway shows, the zoo, or just to her favorite diner, Slims, for lunch; laughing constantly, in a way she laughed with nobody else.

A constant participant in every life event, from my birth to the birth of my daughter Lily; every festive holiday; every high school performance; everything that I can ever remember.

A constant contributor, helping me out whenever she could, however she could, just for the pleasure of seeing me happy or experiencing my success.

Grandma Esther, you provided me with so much wisdom, so much joy, so much love, so much support during your life, and you did it constantly. There is something very reassuring about something so positively constant in your life. Even in death, Grandma, you will remain in my life, constantly.